Annette lives in Wiltshire and has businesses in Bath. She lives with her husband Adrian. They have three grown up children: Angelique, Dominic and Alice between them.

Annette has written this book because she wanted to step over a massive fear of the written word and show how a dyslexic's mind works. Her aim is to change the education system so dyslexics can be taught in a different way to encourage their skills.

Dyslexia Rules KO

Annette Dolan

Dyslexia Rules KO

Vanguard Press

VANGUARD PAPERBACK

© Copyright 2016
Annette Dolan

The right of Annette Dolan to be identified as author of
this work has been asserted by her in accordance with the
Copyright, Designs and Patents Act 1988.

A CIP catalogue record for this title is
available from the British Library.

ISBN 978 178465 142 8

*Vanguard Press is an imprint of
Pegasus Elliot MacKenzie Publishers Ltd.*
www.pegasuspublishers.com

First Published in 2016

**Vanguard Press
Sheraton House Castle Park
Cambridge England**

Printed & Bound in Great Britain

Thank you.

To my husband for editing.

To our children: Angelique Williamson, Dominic Doherty and Alice Dolan.

My niece, Matilda Adlington.

And mostly to my mother, Dorothy Adlington, Brother, Jim Adlington, and my beautiful sister, Rita Adlington, who sadly passed away during the production of this book.

Chapter one

Getting a Job in an Office

'Dust off your dreams hidden deep inside' were the words that hit me most whilst reading the amazing book *The Monk Who Sold His Ferrari*. These words resonated deeply. It also said: 'Connect with your dreams that you had as a child or a young adult.' Well my dream was to be a journalist which was totally ridiculous as I am dyslexic. I have always wanted to write a book and have had many attempts over the years. Due to my experience at school I was ashamed of what I wrote and when I read it back it would fill me with dread and disgust. Now I realise that I am worthy and actually quite clever, I run two businesses and have been successful in most things I have put my energies into.

If only I had realised this as a child or as a young adult. That is why I want to share my experiences through this book now and show any dyslexic people that it can be done, through showing them my life journey to a positive and successful life. It is often the case that dyslexics have been fed a negative mantra of being told you are stupid, dumb, thick, a dunce and ridiculed in front of their classmates. This is often far from the case, as most dyslexics have high IQs. This is still happening in far too many young dyslexics' worlds today as I have discovered with my young dyslexic niece and several people I have interviewed for this book.

When I was at school I tried really hard and would present my work with great pride. No spell check on laptops or specialist software on PCs, as we know today we had no computers in schools in the '70s, just paper, pens and dictionaries. After enduring numerous occasions in the classroom of total humiliation being knocked down so much, I stopped trying. I now know that scared me. I still go hot under the collar when someone asks me which art college did you study at. Then I rationalise it in my head.

Early man did not read or write or even need to, this has developed through time and necessity and we, the humans, have evolved in the world which has developed as we know it today. So all of our systems are man-made with tests to find out how much we know, some people can transfer knowledge onto paper, some cannot. The fundamental thing in life is to feed ourselves, have shelter and care for our offspring. But mankind has made it more than that, we generally measure each other by our wealth, by having things we do not need. Which come to the people who can transfer knowledge onto paper and then through a career. But there are some of us who have a knowledge which is vast and is processed differently. We are the ones who have to find a different way, our own business or lots of unskilled jobs. My school took away any confidence I had and gave me a tainted view of establishment and an inferiority complex, which in a strange way gave me my fighting spirit. As I was going to prove I could succeed whichever way.

At school I would present my work and it would be returned to me covered in 'insults', dashed in red pen across the pages with lines sprawling across my words as though they had no meaning (just like the cover of this book). I used to look at this and it filled me with shame and embarrassment even though I had tried so hard and taken such care. I would cry alone in my bedroom feeling that I was a failure. I did the best I could. I was devastated. So I developed techniques of not doing work and therefore I was no longer a target for the battering ram of the teacher's ignorant irritability. It was easier to just get a telling off for not doing homework, which of course, was much cooler with classmates. After the reprimand nobody really bothered as the teachers always then focused their attention on the 'non-dyslexics'. I loved art and was good at it and regularly got high marks. I loved my art teacher Miss Holland. She encouraged me and told me I had a talent. I loved painting and was always making collages out of magazines in my bedroom.

When I first worked in London I would often visit the National Gallery in Trafalgar Square and stare at the paintings for ages. I had copied the 'Old Man in a Chair' by Renoir at school and my mother was so proud of it she sent it to her sister in Australia. This meant a lot to me. One day as I was on my way to Charing Cross making my way home, diving in and out of the shops in Oxford Street as I often did, I came across a tin handbag decorated with the work of the masters, it was beautiful. I was smitten! It was shaped like an old-fashioned, American sandwich box/ doctor's bag. I had to have it!

On writing this I no longer self-loath my words when I read them back and I am proud of my achievements. In fact, I am writing this with glowing pride. I have written so many books in the past, some of them I destroyed, as I felt a shame and disgust when I read them back. I have stepped through some sort of barrier with this book. Which is one of my greatest achievements because I actually like my writing and no longer feel shame. I am not a dunce as I was told at school and I reiterate, neither are you if you are dyslexic, you are, undoubtedly, very clever.

As I said before, a large proportion of dyslexics have high IQs, great imaginations and often write better stories than non-dyslexics. We are usually good verbal storytellers, but often unable to clearly transfer our thoughts to paper.

I am going to take you through my life and show you how I got to where I am today. We all have unique talents and we need to find them. One of my talents is delegation and as a dyslexic it is a skill which is very useful. If you cannot do something you can find someone to do it for you and eventually you can pay them for their time. This book is a perfect example, as I have written it in my unique manner. There is always someone who has the skills you lack who would be willing to earn money. I will pay them and I will choose very carefully. Firstly, though, I must overcome my gut wrenching fear and submit it to a few publishers.

So, back to my story. I will start at age fifteen when I was at school in South London having moved from Bristol when I was eleven. That was an interesting experience as I had arrived in the depths of South East London from the heart of the West Country with a strong Bristolian accent and long blonde hair which my mum had put into two plaits. One of my first horrific experiences was of a loud-mouthed South London girl coming up to me on my first day and aggressively pushing me in the chest and saying, "Are you fucking Swedish?"

"No!" I replied, innocently, in a broad Bristolian accent, "I'm from Bristol."

"Where's that?" she asked, sneering at me and within seconds punched me to the ground and started to lay into me. It was a very tough school and being from the West Country and dyslexic in South London in the 1970s, in fact it was a disaster. I was so upset and frightened. My accent was so strong I made the decision to change it as quickly as I could to fit in and survive.

All was not lost though as I made good friends with Janice Bavin, Paula Lake and Susan (Susan Ballion, who later became Siouxsie Sioux of the '70s punk band The Banshees). I became a good fighter as I was picked on constantly, and eventually the challenges stopped.

In those days a girl would challenge me to a fight, then word got round the school and there would be a ring of people waiting for the fight to happen after school. They would all chant "Fight... fight...fight!" First there would be the pushing and shoving then reluctantly I would release my anger and frustration through my fists as they landed accurately and painfully in the other girl's face.

I always won as it didn't take long for the white anger to come out. I was sad and so angry about being picked on and the fact that my second dad had cancer; also I had not seen my real dad since I left Bristol. My brother Jim used to threaten anyone at his boy's school, Edgebury, just down the road and say that if they picked on him his sister would get them.

I had built a reputation for being a good fighter. One time a particular fight with a particularly tough girl who had a mini gang who were all quite hard too, there was the usual ring of school kids waiting outside the school gates: her gang, for Jan and me. It was agreed I would fight the gang leader and Jan would hold my cookery tin containing the results of my hard work in home economics, a fruit trifle

After the usual initial pushing and shoving my red anger proved too much for the gang leader and I won again, leaving her with a thick lip and bloodied nose. I had proved my point.

Relieved it was all over Jan and I started walking home with our cookery tins safely under our arms and me adjusting my torn shirt and school tie. Suddenly Jan got a burst of confidence

"Chickens…!" she shouted back at them, thinking we were a safe distance away

"What did you do that for? There's five of them… run!" I shouted as I could see them turn and start charging towards us.

I was a great runner, always came first on sports day. Jan wasn't bad either and we managed to make it to the woods and hid avoiding a heavy beating but sadly the fruit trifle didn't!

So as word got round the challenges eventually stopped.

On the last day of school it was tradition that everyone signed your shirt and then the non-leavers ripped them off. So walking home with Janice on the last day of school in ripped shirts reflecting on what we were going to do with our lives. We had walked that route so many times sharing our emotions; it was a sad day. When we were younger we used to go on the rope swing over the stream.

Janice, who always called me Nettles, said, "Nettles, shall we have one last go on the rope swing?"

"Why not?" I replied.

So we raced through the woods laughing and jumped on the rope swing together. We started to swing back and forth. Of course we had grown since the last time.

'Snap!'

The rope broke, we fell and I landed on top of Jan in the stream.

She was laughing hysterically and said through breaths of laughter.

"I hope I haven't broken my back!"

Luckily she was fine. We both arrived home soaking wet.

That night we went to the Lyceum Ballroom in the Strand and danced wildly to Alice Cooper's 'Schools Out'. We felt Alice Cooper was singing just for us.

Jan and I used to go to the Lyceum Ballroom on Mondays – it was for sixteen to eighteen year olds. It was great, we used to dance like mad. There was one problem, being only fifteen we had to quote our date of birth to get in. Jan was very good at this I would always be overtaken by nerves so we used to practise it all the way on the train. By the time I had walked to the Lyceum from Charing Cross it had gone. One time we had to go home because I fluffed it.

Janice met her husband, Dave, at the Lyceum – he was from Hammersmith – when they were fifteen. At that time we were both virgins and had a promise that the first one of us who did it (as we expressed it then) would tell the other one if you felt or looked different. Most of the girls at school had "done it" as we so eloquently put it and had told us all about it. They called Jan and I 'the virgins of Mottingham'.

When Janice eventually knew Dave was the one, she phoned me on the auspicious morning after.

"Hello, Nettles, guess what…? I've done it!"

I gasped, "Noooo…! You haven't, have you? Have you looked in the mirror? Do you look different?"

Jan giggled. "I don't know," she replied.

"What was it like?" I asked impatiently.

"It was lovely."

I knew that that day I lost my best friend to the love of her life.

I felt sad and lonely but happy for her. Jan was my confidant and my life.

I always was insanely jealous of Janice's writing at school. It was always neat with rounded letters. She always got ticks. We were very different. I was wilder than her; she was neat in her dress sense.

My mother was always saying, "Why are you not like Janice? She is still neat and tidy at the end of school day, you look like you've been dragged through a hedge backwards."

Later on we would confess to each other. Jan said she wanted to be more like me and I wanted to be like her. We really laughed. I still love Jan to this day.

By the time I reached the age of fifteen I had learnt the art of survival and was a lot tougher than when I first arrived in London. With my total lack of academic results I was asked to leave school at the age of fifteen. So with no choice but to quit education I went out into the big wide world. When I look at fifteen year olds now they are so young.

So a week before the leaving date I was sent to a careers advisor. I walked into her office. She had a file with my name on the front. I sat down in front of her and she looked at me. "What do you want to do?" she asked.

"I want to be a journalist," I replied positively and enthusiastically.

She looked at my file and laughed. "You're joking, you can barely read and write," she said mockingly.

I glared at her.

"I can read," I insisted, feeling insulted, "and I can write, I just can't spell!"

She looked at me irritated.

"Your only hope is getting a job in Woolworths," she said disparagingly, and threw an application form across her desk at me. I threw it straight back.

"I'll get a job in an office then," I exclaimed.

"You have no qualifications. How you will get a job in an office?" she asked.

That was her gift to me. I would invent qualifications for a job. After another vote of no confidence from her I got up. "You just watch me!" I exclaimed and stormed out slamming the door.

I was glad to leave school because as a dyslexic it was a place of constant negative input, which I was determined to fight as I had been ridiculed in front of the class on so many occasions. I needed to prove I was worthy in life.

It was also a good time for me to leave school as my stepfather was dying of asbestosis and getting a job enabled me to bring a little money in to help my mum.

After reading a lot of self-help books I now think, looking back that as a teenager, I was a positive visualisation natural. I visualised myself working in an office in London. So off I went to central London and bought the *Evening Standard* which was the newspaper that was going to feature in the mapping of my new life. It was an excellent source for job searching.

I applied for a job in Park Street with a company called Gonzalas Byass, a sherry maker and distributor. I was so proud I got the job. Although I do not condone lying, I added a year to my age and put on my application form I had English language, maths and history CSE. I could spell those, but could not spell geography so I never gave myself that one.

That was the gift the very judgmental careers advisor had given me, to pretend I had qualifications. I had interviewed confidently, I had decided that was the only way. I truly had to believe in myself because no one else seemed to.

I not only got the office job but I was in the computer department which in the '70s was cool. Computers were not developed then like they are today. I was employed as a punch card-puller. So I was given a paper invoice which listed the sherries, if it said 2 Tio Pepe or 1 Concha I would pull the punch cards which had been programmed with their details and they would then go to the key punch operators who would input information on them. Then they would go into the big computer in the room next door which sorted them and produced paperwork to work from. This created an order with the right amounts in for the packers to fulfil the orders.

We were only allowed in the 'computer room' with the manager. It was a clinical futuristic room. The computer was taller than me. It was like a scene from a James Bond movie. It was completely white. If I remember rightly we wore white gloves when entering the room to avoid dust getting into the computer. It made a whirring clunking noise. Computers were something out of reach of ordinary people in those days only for experts in the technology. I love technology today as for a dyslexic it helps so much, and opens up worlds and opportunities that we never had back in the '70s.

Gonzalas Byass was a lovely company to work for and it was in a lovely Georgian house two minutes from Marble Arch, so I was just round the corner from Selfridges and Oxford Street.

Shopping was a dream. I felt so grown up. Sometimes on a Friday we would be invited to the tasting rooms at the top of the building. We got to taste the sherries. I loved the taste of the Tio Pepe best, it was a crisp light sherry.

My stepfather died in the third week of my new job, this was so upsetting. He had worked with asbestos for a company called Essex Installation and his team had lagged Battersea power station with airborne asbestos with no masks. Everyone on his team died. He was a lovely man and embraced us as his own. So losing another father was tragic.

I remember my brother, Jim, on the day we were told he had passed. The pain in his eyes was unbearable.

I blamed myself as I had previously written dyslexically on Tom's, my stepfather, cigarette packet, 'giv up smockking it kils you'.

He shouted at me.

"If your gonna write something on my packets make sure you can spell it!"

I did it because I was frightened he would die and I would lose him and if he stopped smoking he would live.

Jim always jokes now it's bad enough losing one dad but to lose two is careless! It is his way of coping with the pain.

My stepfather, Tom, had an amazing sense of humour. Near the end of his life, one of the nights we went to visit him in Grove Park Hospital all of a sudden a gospel singer came into the middle of the ward and started singing at the top of her voice to the ward patients.

"I've got the whole world in my hands…"

Tom said "That's bloody wonderful… we are all lying here dying and she's singing 'I've got the whole world in my hands!'" We all laughed until we cried.

My mother was broken when he passed away.

One minute we were a family, then she was a single mum alone again. Tom loved her; she was the best she ever was with him. She said he was the true love of her life, being philosophical she said she was sent to look after him. They laughed a lot together, another time when he was being cared for at home in bed upstairs he called to my mother "DOT DOT!"

She shouted up, "What is it?"

"I can hear heavenly music, the angels are coming," he cried out anxiously. My mother who was in the kitchen with the radio blaring knew it was the song playing, with the bagpipes playing 'Amazing Grace'. She went up and held his hand. He looked at her. "Why are you not worried I am going?" he said, noticing she had no anxiety.

"It's the radio, you silly bugger." They laughed for ages about that.

My real dad had left my mum for another women when I was five and my brother Jimmy was three. My mother struggled through bringing us up as my father never paid a penny of maintenance. She saved hard for us to have a holiday at Butlins in Minehead. That's where she had met my second father Tom, a cockney. They fell in love and we soon moved from Bristol to London. He had a daughter called Rita who I shared a bedroom with, who I love as my sister. She is a beautiful human being. For us all, losing Tom was very hard to handle.

Rita my lovely Step Sister passed away whilst my book was being written. An hour before she died I played 'Annies' song by

John Denver. She had sang it so beautifully to Ade and I three days before. It was an honour to be with her in the last weeks of her life and sharing our memories of being together in the 1970's.

My friends were impressed with my job in computers but I was starting to get bored. I was given a bit of money from my uncle because of the death of my stepdad and after work one night took a copy of the *Evening Standard* to see what jobs were going. Turned to 'situations vacant' and saw an advert 'models wanted'. It was Lucy Claytons, a modelling agency in Bond Street which offered training in all aspects of the trade. I phoned up and made an appointment. The next night after work I went to Bond Street for an interview. A sleazy looking man and women interviewed me and convinced me if I paid ninety pounds they would train me to be a successful model and the world would be my oyster. It happened to be the exact amount that my uncle had given me when Tom had died and so I signed up, I was excited because being a model you did not need to have good qualifications.

That night I told my mother excitedly that I had signed up for a modelling course. To say she went ballistic was an understatement. At the time my mum worked in the City for the Guardian Royal Exchange group as a telephonist, so after work she bombed up to Bond Street to confront them. They told my mother I had signed a legally binding contract, she argued and told them the story about losing my two dads but they showed no sympathy. When she arrived home she told me it was a con but I would have to do it as I had signed on the dotted line

"I'll tell you why I know it's a con," she said. "They tried to sign me up!"

We laughed till we dropped. My modelling career was born.

I forgot to say, as well as being dyslexic, I have dyspraxia, which means I have the tendency to be rather clumsy.

Well here I was Annette, formally known as 'Spanner' (as in the spanner in the works) with my gang on our South London council estate, where I was a tom boy playing cricket, run outs and British bulldog. I have fantastic memories of those long summer holidays playing cricket and just hanging out.

That is until I grew breasts and could no longer compete with the boys. I remember gazing out of the window watching my brother and them play and mourning those days gone by. I could no longer be one of the boys in the gang as they responded to me differently now and I wasn't ready for that. I was lonely and played Leonard Cohen constantly. I bought "songs of love and hate." His face on the cover reminded me of my real dad and the song 'Famous Blue Raincoat' reminded me of the dark nights just before Christmas when as a little girl I would walk through the streets of Bristol and my dad would sing. He always wore a long blue raincoat. I would look up at his handsome face and feel wonderful. I knew every word of 'Famous Blue Raincoat: it is about a cheating man that was my father.

I soon discovered that Lucy Claytons was an upper-class establishment with well to do girls whose family paid for them to do the course. It was like a finishing course for socialites. Luckily I was never really impressed by anyone let alone anyone posh or middle class. The person who had impressed me most at school was my friend Janice who was natural and always herself. She shone with a genuine glow and had an air of: 'this is who I am you can take me or leave me. I am what I am and I am comfortable with that'.

I was really impressed with her way and had worked out very early on that you are what you are and that's OK and this is also very attractive to others. The course included deportment, makeup, and catwalk. The other girls were absolutely lovely to me and we had a lot of fun.

At the end of the course we had to put on a fashion show for friends and family, also it was to be in front of more sleazy people. They announced that one of us would then be picked for a chance to audition for a Tony Curtis film. I felt a bit non-plussed because of my school experiences where I never got picked for anything, being dyslexic and clumsy.

Well in retrospect, I was 'jail bait' and it was the '70s. Much to my shock and surprise I was picked and promptly taken into a room to be interviewed. The boss man told me that Tony Curtis would come and interview me and I could be in his next film. I had a gut feeling that all was not right, which led me not to believe the nonsense which was being spilled out to me. I am glad I behaved as I did. I told him I did not want to be in a film and that I had a modelling job. He got very irritated with me, sent me away and called in the next girl. Who never appeared in a film. Not only did we pay to do the courses but also I think we were allegedly pimped in front of sleaze balls perhaps for their potential use. The 1970s was interesting in that way. Of course I no longer had a modelling job and as I left that night I felt a failure, because their promises were rubbish. It was business and we were the collateral source.

I felt bad not talking to my mum before I signed anything. I forgot to say on the last night I tripped and fell on to the catwalk. The girls and I nearly wet ourselves laughing. So not one to be deterred I bought the *Evening Standard* on the way into work and there it was my next chapter.

CHAPTER TWO

A Real Chelsea Girl

The *Evening Standard* stated:
House Model wanted
High Street Kensington
Must be size 10

The next morning I went to my mobile phone (the telephone box at the end of the road) and got an interview. That evening I got the district line from Charing Cross to High Street Kensington. When I arrived at a big ugly factory building, I was interviewed by a lovely lady with perfect nails. She had been the house model for Chelsea Girl many years but was now PA to Mr. Bernard Lewis one of the Managing Directors of the Lewis Shops Group. This was the holding company for Chelsea Girl.

She measured me and I tried on some clothes and she offered me the job. I was so excited I could hardly breathe, at last I WAS a model. I ran back to the tube station and rang my best friend, then my mum who told me to calm down and take a breath.

I handed in my notice with Gonzales Byass who tried to persuade me to stay. But punch card pulling could not compete with modelling. I was so excited. Chelsea Girl was where I shopped. It was really trendy and reminded me a bit of a mini Biba. I loved that shop. It was in Oxford Circus and was decorated quite dark and moody. All of my friends thought Chelsea Girl was the best shop. Can you imagine how they were when I told them?

The warehouse and offices in High Street Ken as it was known were, as I discovered on my interview, not at all glamorous. The shops were pure glamour for teenagers. It was of course a factory and warehouse. But nevertheless it was fantastic to know how the clothes were chosen and I was the model, size 10, who tried them on.

So far my dyslexia had not stopped me and this time I gave myself English, Maths, History and French CSEs on my application form. I loved my time at Chelsea Girl. Even though it was not at all glamorous the people were lovely. I was there, the clothes peg girl who tried on the clothes when the designers bought in new designs. It was always in Mr Bernard's office, that's what we called him. There was a screen for me to change behind and I would parade up and down in front of him, Alison (the lovely lady with the nails) and Miss Mynkyo the Italian in-house fashion designer and the designer who happened to be presenting the new samples.

They would choose the designs. They then would be sent to the East End factories, who were called the outworkers, where a lot of the clothes for the fashion industry were made in the 1970s. I would be called up to the fashion studio where there were big tables with patterns on them and lots of cutting and sewing going on. Miss Mynkoyo was in charge of the in house designers and designed herself. It was a room full of energy.

I had to stay a perfect size 10. One morning I was behind the screen trying to put on a dress and I couldn't zip up the sample dress.

"Had I put on a bit of weight?" I asked myself, beginning to panic.

I heard Mr. Bernard ask, "What IS she doing?"

Alison appeared behind the screen. "You all right, Annette?"

"No," I replied nervously, "I can't get the zip up."

She looked at me laughing.

Miss Mynkyo shouted from the other side of the screen, "She's puta on the weight, it's that tea trolley I have seen her eating those bars of chocolate."

She was right, I had become quite fond of that trolley and its calorie charged cargo!

Alison held the zip as I eventually came out from behind the screen and showed the dress. I promised to diet.

When the finished dresses were delivered back from the out workers in the East End Miss Mynkyo would pull a size 10 off a rail they had delivered and I would put it on, trying it for size. It was then I learnt what the expression, 'cutting the cloth' meant. Sometimes I could not get into size 10. It would be too small. This time as I was a perfect size 10 again Miss Mynkyo would measure me to confirm my size, after my experience in Mr Bernard's office. I always watched what I ate after that embarrassing experience. Then she would start shouting at them at the top of her voice with her Italian accent.

"You 'ava cutta' le cloth taka dem back and re-size them."

They used to make them smaller so they could make more dresses and more money. But they never got past Miss Mynkyo: she was very thorough.

Alison took me under her wing and looked after me. I looked up to her. She was educated, smartly dressed, not at all clumsy. I would gaze at her with her perfect nails typing on an IBM typewriter. I thought she was so clever and sophisticated being a PA.

I spent hours dreaming I could be a PA. I asked Alison to teach me to type, and she did. I actually forgot I was dyslexic as it had not been an issue in this job.

I loved seeing Alison type on the headed notepaper on the IBM typewriter. She taught me to use tippex, a liquid paper which was so useful then if you made a mistake. My trial pieces were often covered in mounted tippex.

She would go into Mr Bernard's office for meetings with her blotting book full of the perfect letters she had typed and he would sign them. Then she would fold them so neatly. She gave me a go at folding them but I made a hash of it. I would then take them to the postal department for franking.

My mum and I always travelled up to Charing Cross on the train together; we would always be late and running. We were always like a calamity waiting to happen and had several incidents on the way to the station. My mum was quite strung up after all her experiences but her sense of humour always shone through. One morning she was running in front of me looking behind shouting, "Hurry up we will miss the train."

I shouted, "Mum, look where you are going." Too late she fell down a hole that a workman was working in, on top of him thankfully as it was a soft landing. I pulled her out she could not get up through laughing.

Another time we were sitting in a single carriage. It was full and I was opposite her. She started fishing around in her bag and pointed a tampax at me and said, "Would you like a Polo mint." I was so embarrassed I just made eye movements to her. She got more and more irritable. "What's wrong with you do you want a Polo or not?" By then the whole carriage was looking at the tampax. She looked at them and then the tampax and started laughing hysterically.

Another morning we ran to the platform and Mum jumped on a train. I followed, it was just about to go and she jumped off. I was left on. She had realised it was the wrong train. I watched her mouthing words that I could not hear as the train pulled out of the station. I ended up in Cannon Street. Alison was luckily very understanding.

Mum had taken a job in a pub in the evening so she could meet people, after losing Tom. When you lose people you are vulnerable to superstition. One evening a few months after Tom had passed his friends came to visit: Daphne and John. Daphne looked around the room and suddenly exclaimed that Tom had died because he collected pixies. She said, "They are very unlucky." When they left us, being in a vulnerable state, we grabbed all the brass pixies and put them in bags. By then it was midnight. We then went to our local park: The Foxes, with a shovel and started digging. Half way through the digging my mum stopped and said if anyone came along and asked us what we were doing and we said we are burying brass pixies what would they think? Tears ran down our faces with laughter at the thought. We buried the pixies I still wonder if anyone has ever found them. We laughed about that for years.

I told my mum I wanted to be a PA and got the *Evening Standard* on the way to work and there it was my next chapter.

I was sorry to leave Alison she was so kind to me. She tried to persuade me to stay as we were quite close, but I had to fly.

Secretary/ PA wanted
International Freighting Weekly
Old Burlington Street
London W.1.

Chapter Three

West End Rite of Passage: International Freighting Weekly

This, I thought, was the one for me, my way into journalism. I applied for the job and got an interview. My application form was becoming more impressive at each interview. This time I added English Lit as I thought it would impress the journalistic types. I could not spell the full word so I just put Lit. The interviewer was a really friendly man. He asked me lots of questions and I gave him fantastical answers about being good at typing. He did not give me a typing test and gave me the job.

I turned up on my first day excited, delusional, but proud. He took me to an office with one other girl who was typing with earphones attached to an audio machine. She was typing really fast without looking about sixty words per minute, that's how we measured typing then. I was probably ten words per minute with spelling errors. I sat down on the desk opposite her and the man handed me a miniature tape to put in the audio machine and left. I put the tape in the machine, put the paper in the typewriter and pressed play. The voice of the man rang in my ears: Dear Sir or Madam, I was trying to type but he was talking too fast so I re-wound it. Kathy the girl opposite stopped what she was doing and said you can slow it down, So I slowed it right down it sounded like this: Deeeeearr Sirrr. I had accidentally pressed the loud speaker so there I was with my new boss's voice ringing out in the office and my new boss walked back in.

He looked distressed and looked at my work and said very slowly, "You cannot type, can you?" he asked. "It's my fault, I should have given you a typing test." He was apologising!

I looked at him wide eyed and shook my head.

He continued, "You can't spell either, can you?"

My eyes widened and my head shook faster. I sat there, the careers advisor's words ringing in my ears.

"Stay there! Don't move!" he exclaimed.

So I waited there fearful, that I was now jobless. He came running back into the office with a softly spoken, tall man with glasses called Stephen Taylor.

"This is Stephen," he told me. "He is looking for a girl Friday on *International Freighting Weekly*. Are you interested?"

"Yes," I said excitedly.

A great relief came over his face and Stephen escorted me into the room next door. It was a large room and there were three very good-looking young journalists sitting at their desks. There was a fourth desk with an IBM typewriter on it which was for me. At the end of the room was a door into another room. On it said: 'Stephen Taylor – Editor'.

Stephen introduced me firstly to John who had tumbling, curly locks – a very handsome man.

Then Simon who looked like John Cleese with a long trendy cut who was very public school, posh speaking and then there was Stuart who had a thinning head of blond hair who said, "G' day." He was Australian.

I was very nervous. Stephen took me into his office and explained the job. "You will being filing photographs mostly of juggernauts, ships and ports, typing, making appointments for the boys and booking hotels, and typing my letters."

I looked at him sheepishly and said, "Did the other man tell you I could not type very well and my spelling is terrible?"

Stephen looked at me and smiled. "Don't worry you will learn there is more filing than typing and I will teach you to spell." He was so kind.

I started that day filing pictures of juggernauts and finding pictures to go with stories, answering the phone and all girl Friday duties. Stephen would call me into his office and type the letter on a scrappy piece of paper at ninety words per minute, as most journalists did in those days. He put it in a blotter – a big book full with blotting paper to blot your work. He would hand it to me to type onto headed paper. This still makes me laugh now. I would then proceed to type it onto headed notepaper on an IBM typewriter just like Alison's. I felt so proud as I put my first bit of paper into the typewriter.

I had painted my nails and they had chipped, still I was nearly a PA. I told myself that a girl Friday was nearly a PA. But I was to make mistakes, not to worry, Alison taught me how to use tippex liquid paper. So on my first attempt I had mountains of tippex with letters on the top to the point you could not read the spelling mistake. The bad layout leapt out at me. Why did it not look right? But I still finished it proudly. When I felt it was OK I took it into Stephen who then marked it for me. He gently pointed out spelling mistakes and lay out problems and gave it back to me to do again. This process went on for I think ten attempts until I got it right. I was glowing with pride when he signed it and he showed me how to fold it carefully into the envelope.

On the second day of my new career, I was put under a Spanish inquisition by the boys. 'Where was I from?' 'Did I have a boyfriend?' 'Was I a virgin?' This went on daily.

I loved my new job working with three hunky men who were journalists. John was the coolest as he had worked on *NME* and *Melody Maker* the music newspapers. He talked about his experience meeting lots of people in the music industry. I was a virgin and totally naïve. They had made a bet unbeknown to me, had a bet on which one could de-flower me. I found this out from a girl from Surrey who I used to meet by the photocopier.

She told me of their plot to de-flower me.

I stupidly said, "What does de-flowering mean?"

"To take your virginity!" she advised me.

I returned to the office gingerly and not one for holding back said, "I hear you have a bet to de-flower me," (which was a mistake as it made me look more confident than I really was).

"Yes," said John, nervously. "It was Stuart's idea."

I was secretly pleased I had learnt a new trendy word. I also really found John attractive but I was totally in awe of him: he seemed so hip, clever and handsome.

I think Stephen saw me as a daughter. He was so kind and gentle; he got frustrated with the boys.

First of all they took me out for a drink, all together with others from *Mclean Hunter* which was the parent company of *IFW*, to the Old Burlington Pub at the end of Old Burlington Street. Here they introduced me to serious alcohol consumption as only journalists knew and always tried to get me drunk. Then one by one they asked me out. If my memory serves me right it was Stuart first who took me to see a Barry Humphries film. He was actually a real gent and did not try it on, not even a kiss.

They were all strong characters and I would get quite jealous of their travelling off to their assignments. They were always popping off to Amsterdam or Italy. I remember one day Simon who not only looked like John Cleese but sometimes behaved liked him, throwing all his photographs off his desk and shouting, "THAT'S IT!! Why do I always have to go to fucking Scunthorpe? It's the back of beyond. You two always get the best stories," he shouted at John.

"I went to Derby last week!" John piped up.

Simon then exploded. "You're from fucking Derby, you went to see your folks!!" in a loud public schoolboy accent, and stormed out. Stephen calmed the situation down. The next assignment that landed on Simon's desk was Grimsby. I started laughing nervously as Grimsby sounded a far worse place than Scunthorpe from the 'Grim' proceeding the 'by' of it. He looked at me and started laughing uncontrollably.

I said between laughter, "I wish I could go to Grimsby I am always stuck here."

He laughed. "No one wants to go to Grimsby!" The next day he was on his way to Grimsby.

I carried on typing five to ten letters to Stephens's one perfect one on scrap paper. Idly staring at John I would dream he would whisk me off my feet like a knight in shining armour, the way sixteen-year-old virgins do.

Simon was the next to ask me out. We went for a quiet drink in the Old Burlington mid-week which was interesting. He was also a really nice person, and didn't make a move on me.

Finally John asked me out. I was so excited and felt so grown up as he took me to a restaurant in Greenwich by the river. It was beautiful. The lights sparkled on the water. We had a lovely meal on a terrace over the Thames, and then he asked me back to his flat in Forest Hill. To me for someone to have their own flat was so impressive. He had one of those massive sideways music tape reel-to-reel machines which he must have needed when he worked for *New Musical Express*. This was pre-CD players: it was like a giant sideways reel-to-reel cassette with no cover. It looked very impressive to me, the sort of thing you would only see in a music studio.

"I want to play you some Monkees," he said, "stuff that no one has heard, they're actually quite good musicians."

"OK! But can I just use your loo?" I asked.

When I came back into the room, I stood there, frozen with shock. I had expected to hear the Monkees playing and mugs of coffee on the table. But John was standing in front of his futuristic tape machine stark naked with a massive erection! I had only ever seen a penis in the bath when my brother was three.

Well! I stared at him open-mouthed. 'This is not what I wanted,' I thought to myself. I had never seen an erect penis before, I was terrified. He slapped me around the face.

"Why had I agreed to go out with him?" he asked.

"Because of love," I offered rather naively and began to cry.

He apologised profusely, grabbed his clothes looking very embarrassed holding them close to him.

Through my sobs I explained I had not seen a naked man before and this was quite a shock. He passed me the coffee he had made earlier and then took me home.

He came in and sat rather nervously and had a cup of tea with me and my mum. I said nothing to her I was so embarrassed. That night I lay awake worrying about how I would face him the next day in the office. I had said the 'love' word to him. My mind was

34

going mad, he must think I am stupid, he is so cool. The ironic thing was I still liked him. I felt so immature, which of course I was.

I was braver than I thought. I got up the next morning and told my mother I was ill and couldn't possibly go into work. She was not having any of it, dragged me up to the train station, kept asking me what was wrong. "Nothing," I said.

"You're not bored with this job already," she said irritably.

"No, I love it." She left it at that.

I mustered up the courage to open the office door my heart racing, and to my surprise everything was normal. Stephen called me in for letter writing and the day passed with no hitch. I avoided eye contact with John but secretly I adored him more now. But felt unworthy of him because he could write beautifully – he was a journalist, I was just an illiterate girl Friday who could not even finish a letter in one go. They all typed word perfect.

I stayed at IFW for a year before the boredom set in. I was probably typing three letters to Stephen's one by then, even sending telexes then, that's how we communicated to people overseas those days. We only had letters or telexes to do this. I was also still swooning over John who was patronisingly kind to me after our experience. He obviously realised I was still quite childlike.

I was jealous of the boys' worldwide travelling and looked in the *Evening Standard* for jobs abroad. I chatted to the girl from Surrey on the photocopier who said, "Why don't you try *Lady* magazine. There are always jobs for au pairs abroad in there. So at lunchtime, full of excitement, I ran out of the office in search of *Lady*. Bought a copy and there it was, my next chapter.

'*Au Pair Needed – Milano*

Must be good with children'

I went to my then mobile phone, the telephone box, and called the number.

Chapter Four

Milano Sept 1973

The interview was in a very upmarket hotel next to Harrods, Kensington (which my mother always called it H A Rodds which made it sound like a plumbers, as a joke), which always made me laugh. The lady who interviewed me was called Guggio Radice Fossati. She was very slim and beautiful with long blonde hair and a very kind face. She explained the job was looking after her four children and a little housework.

She was studying archeology at Milano University. The pay was good and it was a living in position. She asked me if I was good with children. I told her I had practically brought up my brother, which was totally untrue as he was only two years younger than me. I had no application form to fill in; she was not worried about my exam results.

She offered me the job.

I had no passport and I had only ever flown twice on temporary ones with my friend Paula to Spain and Italy. I went home excited and gave the news to my mum.

"You're not going!"

A massive row broke out.

"You can't stop me!"

She said she could but in the end, after much screaming and shouting, she conceded and said only if she could meet the family before I went. I agreed.

Still at Mclean Hunter I was organising everything in my lunch hour. I finally got my passport and carried it around in my bag everywhere. I was so excited and proud of my black passport.

In those days, as I look back, I was still a child and loved to run everywhere to the station, to the shops or to get my sandwich at lunchtime. This particular lunchtime I ran out of Mclean Hunter, turned left then ran straight in to a man dressed in a Kaftan outfit and fell at his feet. As he picked me up I looked into his face. It was Rod Stewart.

Being totally sixteen, I just screamed, "You're Rod Stewart!"

He was with another man dressed in a suit.

"Yes... sure I am but what's the hurry?" he replied.

I looked at him and spurted out, "I always run... can you sign something? Otherwise my friends won't believe me."

"Yes," he said.

I frantically reached into my bag and out came my passport. He signed one of the inside pages.

"Thank you! Thank you!"

As I ran on he shouted after me, "Slow down life's worth living."

I sat back in the office and showed the boys my shiny new passport with Rod Stewart's signature. I must say they were really impressed.

This got me in real trouble with customs as on my way to Italy the customs officer saw the signature.

"What's this?" he asked fiercely.

"It's Rod Stewart's signature!" I replied proudly.

"You and Rod Stewart should know better," he shouted.

"But it's my passport," I protested.

"No it's not. It is a document of the realm. Do not get any more famous people to sign your passport," he said sternly.

The word celebrity did not exist then. I apologised and went through to the boarding lounge.

I had no fear. I was excited about my new job abroad. I was now travelling like the boys. I had decided I did not want to be a commuter all my life. If that careers officer could see me now.

Guggio, the Italian lady, met me at Milan Airport. I was shocked by the September heat which hit me as I got off the plane. As we drove from the airport I noticed it was so different from England. There was no grass – it was very barren from the hot sun.

She drove into a lay-by which had a melon stand. I had never seen a melon before. It was a water melon and was so delicious and thirst quenching. I realise now looking back I really was still a child myself then, but I felt so grown up. Also looking back I was learning new things about life all the time. Education is not just about words and numbers; it is also about experience.

Communication: it is the key to business, sales and delegation is a key thing missing from the curriculum for dyslexics.

We drove through the outskirts of Milan which is very industrial and arrived at a very exclusive apartment in central Milan. It was via Elvatia 18. I learnt that road name off by heart as any Italian would say it. There were electric gates just like in a James Bond movie. Guggio drove us into an underground car park and we took a lift to the penthouse apartment. The street was beautiful as it faced the Castello (Milan's castle) with parkland and many trees by it.

When we arrived in the apartment I was introduced to four very attractive children. The eldest was Angelica, then Barbra, then Paulo and the youngest as cute as could be who was just over one, Micele. Micele was who I spent most time with. Guggio showed me to my room where I had my own en suite bathroom. The room had a wardrobe and a bedside table. She gave me the low down on what was expected of me and asked me to join them for supper. I unpacked and placed my tin handbag on the bedside table which made me feel at home.

I felt strange. My fantasy of travelling was unravelling into reality. I had a lot of willpower which was not always a good thing.

I settled into life in Milan. The children were being educated at the American School in central Milan so they spoke perfect English. The three older ones were at school daily and I was left to look after Micele who was really cute. They had a frail, older woman called Mary as their cleaner/cook. She worked very hard and was a fantastic cook. I still make her recipes today.

The apartment was big and open plan with a balcony overlooking the Castello (Castle) grounds. The children and I spent a lot of time in the park. My mother phoned daily as she was still a telephonist at the Guardian Royal Exchange Group in the City. This used to make me a bit homesick. I missed her and my brother and my friends. But it was lovely to talk daily.

I had one day off a week and there was an au pair group which Guggio directed me to, where I met a lovely girl from Birmingham called Janet. She had an Anglo/Italian boyfriend.

We had a meeting place every day where all the au pairs would meet for coffee with the little ones.

I started Italian lessons and Janet suggested we go out one night to a club at the opposite side of the Castello grounds called of all things 'The Old-Fashioned Club'. I thought this name hysterical so un-Italian. My first visit was a complete culture shock. There was a huge dance floor, then an iron ornate fence, then tables encased by another iron encased fence. Then a space like a corridor around that. All the girls sat down and the boys paraded round eyeing up girls. It was truly a cattle market. I told Janet I felt threatened.

"Oh you will get used to it, is the Italian way." Then I went to the loo.

There were English girls chatting, they were saying, "I know he is Mafioso as I felt his gun in his trousers when we were dancing."

This was a whole new world for me.

I told Janet.

"Ignore them they think every Italian boy is Mafioso"

We danced. It was a good night. Janet's boyfriend Alan introduced me to an Italian man. He seemed older so I was not interested. But he kept persisting to ask me to dance. I did not think any more of him.

The older children I looked after were difficult. If I tried to discipline them they would say, "You're not my mummy. I am going to tell mummy of you." She would then appear after work like the angel and never discipline them. I started to enjoy going out with my newfound friends, but Guggio and her husband also wanted to go out a lot, so it was a fight of who would baby-sit, as they too had a busy social life. Luckily Janet told me the au pair union rules, as she joked, my day stops at six p.m.

Guggio was married to Oslo Radice Forssati, an Italian businessman who looked like a Chancellor of the Exchequer type: very serious. I was not used to dealing with men, not having either of my dads for any length of time. I found him intimidating and he found me irritating as a consequence.

Life jogged on as normal. I was enjoying it, but one day normality changed. Mary was ill. I was asked to iron Oslo's shirts, having never ironed a man's shirt before in my life, so I ironed his shirts. The next morning I heard a scream from their bedroom. It was Oslo screaming about the shirts. On some I had totally forgotten to iron a sleeve and on others the collars were missed. He was going mad.

Guggio tried to calm him down but he shouted at me. I was so upset, as I wanted to please him.

The next day Mary returned and taught me how to iron his shirts. There were to be no creases on the arms or the collars. It was a difficult process but I finally mastered it. This made me unhappy, as I had not had a father figure for more than five years and I sought his approval. It devastated me when he criticized me.

One Sunday I really upset him.

As Catholics they went to church as most Italians used to then. I was able to go and meet my friends if I came back and put the Sunday lunch Mary had prepared on. I met my friend in the café. It was fun, but on the way back I realised I had left my key in the apartment. Luckily one of the neighbours came at the same time and let me in the electric gates. So I went up in the lift and saw at the end of corridor was the fire escape door so I went up to the roof to see if I could get down to the balcony. It was very high and dangerous but I was a nimble child and managed to fall down onto the balcony without breaking anything. I tried to open the big glass doors to no avail. Then it dawned on me there was no way back up I was stuck on the balcony so I waited nervously as there was nowhere to hide. I was in full self-conscious view. They came in and they did not notice me. After Guggio called me a few times, one of the children saw me and started pointing and shouting. Oslo looked at me and started waving his hands about and shouting. Luckily Guggio who needed an au pair stayed calm. I got a fit of the nervous giggles and ran to my room, which made it worse with Oslo.

Eventually I sat down to lunch with them and all they kept asking me, "How on earth did you get out there? It looked impossible!"

On my days off I used to go to the Piazza Duomo and meet friends and have lunch in the beautiful Galleria. The Duomo itself is a beautiful cathedral ('duomo' refers to the principal church of a town or city, whatever its status). It was very spiritual and people were always lighting candles.

"Why do they light candles?" I asked my friend.

"It's like a wish," she replied, "for their loved ones."

So I started lighting candles for my mum.

I prayed she would meet someone as she was lonely after losing my stepfather. She had my brother but it's not like a partner. Low and behold she phoned a week later excitedly saying she had met a man. She had gone to a singles club in Bromley with her friend Ann. Alan was his name and, it was also his first night. They did not like the singles club but had agreed to see each other for a drink. I was so pleased.

Also in Piazza Duomo were Italian transvestites. I had never seen them before, they had their own area. They were often very beautiful. I was so astonished. I could not believe they were men.

I had met another friend in the Piazza Duomo, a busker. He was an American with a bad leg. He used to sing *American Pie* to me and we would sit and chat for hours on my days off. He was a member of 'The Children of God sect' and often tried to get me to join. I became very tempted as the children I looked after were behaving like brats and Oslo was getting me down. I agreed to join, but then he said you have to bring all your worldly possessions and donate them to the core of the group, then you will be given clothes and food forever. Well not understanding the concept of Buddhism or any religion I was most indignant. Also bearing in mind I had nothing at all of any value, the thing I did not want to give up most was my tin handbag I had bought in Oxford Street. It was covered in old masters from the National Gallery. I loved it, but I felt they were mine, I had worked for my possessions. They felt special so I refused to join even though my things were worthless.

Then Guggio announced we were off to their country house in Montesolera, a small village near to Lake Como. She said we were going at the end of the month. It turned out to be a country estate with a massive mansion, a church and a farm. When we arrived I was shown to my room. It was beautiful and it had a glorious stone floor, an antique bed, shuttered windows, antique Italian furniture and a view to the Alps. There was snow at the top of them. I can still see the view in my mind's eye now. All of the extended family came: Guggio's brothers and sisters and their children, maids and butlers. I did not have a lot to do there but play with the children. I lunched with the servants and dined with

44

the family. It was weird because the man I had lunch with was serving me with white gloves in the evening. But I was happy. I loved the countryside. It was an old Italian village near to Lake Como.

I ventured out one day on my own on my day off. I walked through the little streets with ancient houses and saw lacemakers dressed in black outside their houses. I watch their fingers move at a great speed, the bobbins forming beautiful lace in front my eyes. My Italian was getting better so I was able to talk to them a bit. It was fascinating. I asked Guggio at dinner why they wore black. She told me because they were widowed and a widow would never wear colour again. Guggio also told me that her handsome brother was getting married, did I have something to wear? I explained to her I had a dress which my next-door neighbour made for me for my dad's funeral. "That sounds good," she said.

On the day of the wedding I got ready in my beautiful room and walked along the stone floor to the stairs, everyone was at the bottom of the stairs. Oslo caught my eye and whispered something angrily to Guggio. Everyone was in their finery and I was in, to be quite honest, a very frumpy dress. I felt awful. I carried on and travelled to the wedding with the servants. We arrived in a lovely Italian village. The church was ancient, the bride looked stunning and the groom wore a navy blue jacket with very long tails and a grey cravat. All of the children were dressed in light blue, they looked great.

The reception was at a mansion bigger than Villa Radice Forrsati where I was staying, with a lake and monuments in the garden. I think we stayed in Montsolero until mid-October because upon our return I remember the leaves on the trees of the Castello were autumnal, it looked stunning.

The week before we left Montesolero all of Guggios' relatives had gone and they closed the main house and I was moved into another bedroom. It was awful as at night rats ran over my bed. I was terrified. I told Guggio who said, "Borrow one of Signora Vingnatie's cats."

Now Signora Vingnaties lived on the estate all year round. She was a very old lady who looked like a witch with millions of cats. So I went to see her. She gave me a cat who came to my room. I got no sleep as the cat fought with the rats all night. I was so glad to leave for Milano.

As I said the Castello grounds were stunning and the children and I used to love going around them on our bikes .My mother used to call me and scream down the telephone, "Is that woman mad letting you loose in Milan with four children on bikes!"

I would calm her down and say it was fine.

"Doesn't she know how accident prone you are?" she would protest.

Then Guggio would chat to her and calm her down.

I returned to Milan and was going out with Janet and Alan, her boyfriend, who said that the man I had met before, called Georgio, wanted to take me out. I still wasn't ready for boyfriends. I had one called Kenny but as I refused to sleep with him he dumped me just after my stepfather had died. I was devastated. He was not a nice person. Anyway back to Georgio, he was a typical Italian what we would call a wide boy and he had a gun. (I did not know about his gun initially.) I was not interested which made him more interested.

One night at home in the apartment babysitting the door phone went. I picked it up. It was Alan and Georgio drunk.

"What number are you in?" they asked.

"Go away," I replied.

I don't know how they got in. I begged them to go away knowing that Oslo would go mad. Ten minutes later there was a knock on the door to the apartment. Luckily there was a door chain so I managed to half open the door.

"Annette…! Please go out with me!" he begged. "Please… go out with me! Please…!"

He went on and on so much I eventually gave in and agreed so long as he would go away and I wouldn't get into trouble with Oslo if I had these two drunks in the apartment.

So that's how I agreed to go out with him. He took me to a good restaurant in his white sports car speeding across Milano. Then speeding on the way home he was stopped by the police. Not only did they get him out of the car, they split all his seats, found drugs in his seats and a gun on his dashboard and arrested him. I just stood there in shock.

The police took me back to Via Elvacia 18. I was so scared. Then I realised my passport had been stolen. My passport with the lovely Rod Stewart's signature on the inside page. I never saw Georgio again or my passport.

Janet and Alan apologised and said they didn't realise he was Mafioso and a drug dealer. I went to the police station the next day to see if they had found my passport. The policeman said that they hadn't and kept asking me on a date.

It was infuriating. He persisted and I told him no twenty times.

I eventually got the right paperwork to take to the consulate so that I could at last get a temporary passport.

As time went on I got tougher with the Italian men. I had one literally follow me around Piazza Duomo. He was a foot shorter than me and insisted I had my photograph taken with him. I had to shout at him to go away in the end.

I returned to a routine two nights a week at the Old-Fashioned Club and looking after the kids and never saw Georgio again. I think he went to prison.

Then Guggio announced we were going to Verbier skiing for Christmas. Being so young I was getting more and more homesick and when my mum called that day I got really upset. Guggio who was so lovely suggested that I go to Verbier early December but she would pay for a ticket for me to return home to England at Christmas. I accepted her generous gift which then gave me a target to see my family again. Living with someone else's family is hard as a job, you always feel like an interloper. We discussed it often amongst the au pairs at the café where we all met. We all felt like family together all being strangers to the country.

Guggio was excited about Verbier. She said it was a great journey as we were going to drive through the Grande Bernard Tunnel which took us right under the mountains. I of course had never skied before.

We went to Verbier and two days before Christmas the chauffeur drove me back through the tunnel and dropped me at Milan Airport. He was a lovely guy and we chatted in Italian all the way. I was getting quite good.

The plane journey back was horrendous and actually put me off flying. I boarded the plane where there were quite a few Italian

48

nuns settling into their seats. I sat next to one, everything proceeded as normal but as we flew over the Alps… disaster! Suddenly the plane dropped. I don't know how many feet it just dropped. Without warning the lights went out. My stomach felt like it was in my mouth.

The nun was screaming, "TUTTI MORTO! MORTO!" (We are all dead!)

I did not move. I sat there holding on to my seat with my knuckles white in abject fear. The nun continued screaming and it went through my head that she did not seem to have the connection with the universe or God.

The lights came back on I stayed frozen, breathing deeply. Then I cried real tears when it was all OK again. We then went through another not quite so bad bit of turbulence and I breathed deeply again. Eventually we arrived at Heathrow and I was never so relieved to get off a plane as I was that time. I have flown again but never experienced anything as bad as that. After that I suffered a severe fear of flying.

I had a lovely Christmas with my mum and brother Jim. I raved about Italian food to them and bought back a Panettone, the traditional Italian Christmas cake. My mum got upset as she thought I was complaining about her cooking. But I wasn't. I had discovered new tastes and different ways of cooking. In those days Italian food was just coming to England. We had not ventured from the spaghetti Bolognese which was the chic thing in the sixties. My mum used to have spaghetti Bolognese evenings with her friends, with a bottle of Matteus Rose. Italian sandwich shops were popping up all over London, also restaurants. I remember going to an opening of one in Piccadilly and feeling very grown up eating lasagne which I had never heard of before. Burning my mouth on the first mouthful.

I left to go back and a white knuckle flight back to Milan. I adopted a constant white knuckle flying technique thereafter. This was basically about grabbing the seat and sitting stiffly in the seat until landing. I did not want to stop flying but it terrified me, until a few years ago I flew to New York with my son Dominic many years after my turbulence experience. On the way back from the Big Apple I was sat in my white knuckle flying position, hands firmly clenched to the seat, eyes fixed. Another passenger in the next aisle looked at me and smiled and in the most dulcet of Irish tones said, "Have you got a fear of flying?"

I looked at him wide eyed. "How do you know?"

Again his beautiful soft Irish voice. "I can tell by the way you're clutching the seat." He laughed.

I told him my story of my Italian flight and how I rationalise it in my head now to actually get on the plane, but the feeling still comes over me. He explained to me gently that he was a healer and did a lot of work in war zones with sufferers of traumatic stress disorders. He explained that he didn't heal the mind but the body which also holds memories. I was confused and asked him to explain more. He told me that there is a level of memory in your body and no matter what you do with your thoughts, this cannot clear the body memory.

I was fascinated. I had flown a lot since but not been able to get rid of the feeling. He then asked if I would mind if he healed me. I told him that would be fine but I did not understand how he could. My son Dominic was witness to this and had often despaired with embarrassment at my distressed flying techniques, screaming out loud as the plane left terra firma if it was a rough take off and asking the staff if all doors were secure, (which I saw was suggested on a website for those with a fear of flying).

As the plane began preparing for take off, he gently placed his hands on me in several places and went into a trance-like state.

I tell you quite honestly that I have never ever feared flying since that day. I feel honoured to have met this lovely gentle man whose name I've never known. His face was open and real, his voice was like an Irish angel and his presence was as calming as anybody I have ever met. I sat and relaxed into the rest of the flight and my son Dominic chatted to him happily about Ireland and his experiences. Both Dominic and I often marvel at that experience.

I went back to my job in Italy which required no reading or writing but lots of emotional stamina. (Nobody explained that need at school to me.) The chauffeur picked me up at Milan Airport and we drove back through the Grande St Bernard to Verbier.

Verbier in 1973 was a beautiful little skiing resort, frequented by the rich.

I can honestly say I was missing all the grandious world. As I was just caught up in my own little world of trying to make my way in an interesting fashion, as I found mundane things boring and wanted to feel the world. I also had a bizarre thirst for knowledge. I was interested in art, buildings and anything I found fascinating. That thirst was not quenched at school as I could not learn in a conventional way. Teaching dyslexics so desperately needs to be reviewed.

The apartment was a typical skiing chalet with lots of bunk beds. I was left holding the baby. I did not mind as this was of course my job.

I met really nice German au pair who also had a care of a baby and enjoyed being in the mountains, it was stunning. I tried skiing but was useless, but I can ski relatively well now and love it.

We returned to Milan for the school term and I resumed my position there. One night Guggio said that we were going to visit a relative on an island called Isola Bella, a very charming island and I needed to wear something smart. Oh no, I thought, here we go again. I'm going to be judged by Oslo. Little did I know that it was going to be worse than that.

We arrived at this amazing place on the island Isola Bello. The house was a mansion with loads of servants and I was sat at a table that could only be compared with what might be seen at Buckingham Palace: white linen, sparkling crystal glasses and line upon line of cutlery. I had never seen so many knives, forks and spoons in one place setting.

Guggio, who was sat next to me, whispered to me that you use you cutlery from out-side in. Which is what I did. My legs were shaking under the table from nerves. Everyone was dressed up to the nines and they all spoke English, some of them I knew from the wedding party. We started eating and then I was subjected to loads of questions: where I came from, where I lived what family I had. I just told them the truth about my upbringing. Then they started talking about table manners. Apparently in Italy as they told me, between courses your hands go on your lap.

"What happens in England?" they enquired.

I was feeling increasingly sick at this point, nervous of my somewhat 'deprived' background.

"I don't know," I offered rather sheepishly sinking into my seat. "At our house we only have one course." They then told me that the English put their hands on the table, or was it the other way around. That was the first time I was subjected to one-upmanship from a wealthy game player type. That stood me in good stead as I came to recognise it later on in life and dealt with it in exactly the way I did then: with honesty. It becomes boring to them then, if you answer honestly. Putting people on the spot is a sport for some insecure people. This is never a good thing for anyone to be subjected too, but for a dyslexic it is worse. If like me you have been through school with little or no support and having had unsympathetic teachers you would already have been subjected to this. Who in the world has the right to judge someone for not having money or experiences?

I did not feel beneath them as I knew I had been brought up by a superstar, Dorothy, my mother who had struggled against all the odds to feed and clothe us after losing one husband to another woman and the second husband three years after she met him to asbestosis cancer. That to me is a class act.

So sitting at that table I felt got at but I did not once feel inferior. Perhaps that is one of the gifts of dyslexia: finding the belief in yourself against the odds and getting that practice at school and the art of failure and continuing anyway. My husband Adrian calls it tenacity. The evening passed and they warmed to me more. I knew Guggio was fond of me. I eventually enjoyed it, again being served with waiters in white gloves just like in Downton Abbey.

Oslo was getting more and more irritable with me, remember I was sixteen and always wanted to be out with my friends and not spending time with them. There were arguments about babysitting on my nights off. I reached a point where I was no longer enjoying being an au pair. On this particular day we were debating who was to go out and I just burst into tears.

"I am leaving," I announced.

"You can't leave, you have nowhere to go," insisted Guggio.

"I can and I have!" I exclaimed. "I'm going to join the 'Children of God'."

"You can't!" she shouted. "I promised your mother I would look after you."

I rushed up to my room, packed my bags and took a bus to Piazza Duomo to find my American friend. He was nowhere to be seen. I asked another busker who told me he had gone back to America. I then remembered my mum was phoning that day and Guggio would have told her by now.

So I found a phone box and called her.

"Annette, please come home," I heard her say. "Make your way to the airport and I will organise a flight."

I sobbed.

"I can't, I'll feel like a failure."

"You not a failure!" she said quietly, encouraging me through my sobbing.

"Guggio wants you back," she continued. "She wants to meet me in London to talk about you coming back."

So I made my way to the airport as my mum organised my ticket. Guggio begged my mother to meet her and begged her to persuade me to come back but she wanted me home and knew me as she put it to Guggio. I would always be a free spirit and I told Guggio, "No I won't be back."

Back in London my mum said that I needed a job. I needed to pay back the air fare.

So I bought the *Evening Standard* and began my next chapter.

Temps wanted
The Challenor Service
Tottenham Court Road
London W2

.

Chapter Five

Finding I Could Sell

Back in London my mum insisted, "You've got to get a job."

I was keen to get back to sensible work where I wouldn't feel like a slave and my time would be my own. If anyone considers being an au pair please negotiate your terms and have them in writing before you start.

So up to Oxford Street. I picked up my old favourite, the *Evening Standard* where I saw there was an employment agency called The Challenor Service, advertising lots of jobs. It was at the end of Oxford Street in the Tottenham Court Road end so off I went to go on their books. By this time my application details had grown.

The interviewer was impressed with me. "Can you sell?" she asked me.

I asked her what she meant as it was a totally new concept to me.

She explained that they had a vacancy there in the actual employment agency and it involved cold calling companies and selling applicants to firms in and around London and also working from the *Evening Standard* to tout for vacancies advertised, to go on our books and find them staff and we charged them for that.

"Yes... I'm sure I can do that," I enthused, eager to jump at the opportunity. Oh by this time I had added Italian to my exam claims on my application form, which I could actually speak quite well.

I started the next Monday. I could not find a bus which went to Tottenham Court Road so I had to walk from Oxford Circus. It was the last office on Oxford Street. It was upstairs not like the Alfred Marks agencies which were all on ground level.

I got the job and loved it, if my careers officer could see me now. I interviewed people with all sorts of qualifications from CSEs to degrees and advised them on careers. I very successfully touted for vacancies, especially when I had good candidates. Which now I know, owning my own business you cannot tell until they have done at least three months of employment

Eventually I was promoted to run the temps department, that is when temporary staff are hired to cover sickness or maternity or loss of staff. This meant I had to go and visit HR managers in companies and broker deals to provide them with temps. The agency had a good communication system and your spelling did not matter as it was mostly coded. It was a card system which worked perfectly, for example, if you interviewed someone there was a secret grading system and also you had to communicate on the card exactly what was discussed so the next person could pick it up and take it straight over. That was both with companies and applicants' cards. I also got commission which was good.

I wanted to pay my mum back for my fare back home from Italy. So I applied for an extra job after work on a Thursday and Friday in the pub opposite 'The Tottenham'. Having never worked in a pub it was quite a daunting but exciting new experience. So over I trotted for my first shift wearing some very high heels.

It was a very busy pub with a really long bar and Thursdays and Fridays were the busiest end of week office drinkers. I tootled around in my high heels, pulling and spilling pints upsetting drinkers, who said I had half measured them as it was not filled to the top. Spilling drinks and adding rounds up completely wrong. One customer shouted at me.

"I had the exact same round before and you're charging me a completely different price!"

The manager heard and took over, then looked at me.

"This is not going to work out, love." So that was it and I was off home, devastated, failed again.

In the office the next day the girls all laughed when I shared my story. There were three girls apart from me, Bunty, a girl from a well to do family, Norleen, an Irish girl from Kilburn and Jill a 'normal' girl. Well Bunty laughed about my experience.

"I know how you can earn some money," she spouted. "I do escorting, what about that?"

I looked at her. "Is that not prostituting?" I asked.

"No!" she reassured me. "You don't have to do anything."

Norleen piped up, "No. You don't have to do anything, you just sit, looking pretty, and have a nice conversation over dinner."

"Could I do that?" I asked naively.

"Yes," said Bunty, "but you have to be eighteen. I'll get you an appointment with my agent and make you up tomorrow to make you look older."

Bunty was really glamorous and quite convincing.

So the next day at five o'clock she made me up and took me to Baker Street for an interview. I say an interview but all I needed to do was to give my name and address and telephone number and I got my first job. The man interviewing was an obvious sleaze ball as he explained when I asked several times, "You don't have to do anything," he reassured me, convincingly. "Just be witty and entertaining. You look beautiful so that's all you need to do."

I trusted Bunty.

He told me that I would need to meet a man with a pork pie hat under the clock of Selfridges at six o'clock.

I asked Bunty, "Will you do my make up again?" She assured me she would.

So the next evening I stood under the clock of Selfridges, looking like a child in make-up and waited for a man with a pork pie hat.

A taxi stopped and a man with a pork pie hat leant out of the taxi.

"Are you Annette?" he asked.

"Yes," I replied.

"Well jump in were going to an Italian restaurant in Soho," he said.

Sitting in the car I looked at him. He looked so old and smelt of mothballs. I think he must have been about eighty. So we headed down Oxford Street and stopped by an Italian restaurant just off Wardour Street. He held the door open for me. I was very nervous. I was greeted by a winking waiter which I found strange. We sat down and I was glad it was Italian. We ordered and we chatted.

He told me of his wealth and asked me about my job, that was OK. I was trying to be interesting and witty, after all that is what I was being paid for. Then when dessert came he started talking about getting me into films.

I said, "I do not want to be in films. I want to be a journalist." So he told me he had his connections to Fleet Street. I looked at him, he looked so old and quite frail. Fleet Street was where all the newspapers were produced in the '70s.

The Italian waiter came with a violin and was winking all the time he was playing. Then the man said after dessert, we can go downstairs to the dance floor and dance slowly together.

'Ugghhh!' I thought. 'Oh my God!' and then I panicked.

"I must go to the toilet," I said, picking up my coat and bag which I had refused to give to the waiter when I came in. My mind was blank with fear as I ran through the first door I came to. I found myself in the kitchen.

I shouted in Italian hysterically, "Dove le sortie." (Where's the way out?) They all started panicking in true Italian fashion. The kitchen was chaos.

"I must leave and not through the restaurant!" I screamed dramatically.

Eventually one of the chefs showed me a window at the far end of the kitchen. I climbed out and ran all the way to Charing Cross looking behind me all of the way. I felt the eighty-year-old man was chasing. Of course he wasn't. I got the first train home and the relief I felt as I took my seat on the train was immense.

I arrived home, walked through the door and my mother clipped me around the ear.

"What have you been doing?" she shouted giving me another clip.

She had the phone in her hand.

60

"I have this man on the phone who said you've lost his best client!"

It took me ages to explain to my mum, it was extra work to pay her back. Eventually she calmed down enough to listen and then she said to the man on the phone, "She's only seventeen."

He put the phone down.

She then assured me there was no rush for me to pay the money back. My escort days were over.

I continued in the job and went out with Norleen and often stayed at her mum's in Kilburn. We used to go to a nightclub in Paddington and dance to Barry White, which is where I met Jean Michel, a half-Corsican half-French boy. He had grown up in Paris. I spoke my little Italian and we developed a language that only we understood.

I was young and fell in love. It was the 1970s and the song 'Voulez-vous coucher avec moi' was in the charts. He used to sing it to me. Young, naïve and in love with this handsome French boy. He had long curly locks. He also bought me the Minnie Riperton record 'Loving you'. It enhanced my affair. He lived in a rented ground floor flat in Sussex Gardens, Paddington. He shared with Didier and Thierry who he had come from Paris with him. I used to stay there a lot, hence I lost my virginity.

I continued working with the employment agency and enjoying it. But one Sunday when Jean Michel and I were lying in the sun in Hyde Park next to the Serpentine, he told me the story of his life. How he was born in a mountain village in Corsica and his parents split up. His dad left him in Corsica with his mum, then when he was seven and his brother was five, his father stole them and took them back to Paris and he grew up with his dad in

Paris. Jean Yves his younger brother grew up with his Gran in Solesmes near Lille in Northern France.

He then told me he was going to do a season in Corsica, because he wanted to find his mum.

"What's a season?" I asked.

"It's when you work for the summer when the tourists come," he explained.

"Where is Corsica?" I asked.

"It's above Sardinia just off the French and Italian coasts."

I became very excited. "I would love to come."

"I would love that too," he said. "The air fare is quite cheap and we can hitch around Ajaccio which is where there is most work. I suggest we pay for a hotel for one week. We should get a job by then."

"What could I do out there?" I quizzed him.

"You could be a chambermaid and then learn French, then you could be a hotel receptionist."

I was so excited.

I spoke to my mum that evening who again said emphatically, "No!"

"Please talk to Jean Michel," I pleaded. "He has it all planned. Please, Mum, I have only just met him and I will lose him!"

By that time Didier and Thierry had returned to France and Jean Michel was living in Notting Hill. It was a bit rougher in those days. He rented from a dirty old English lady with loads of cats. He used to call her Coco Chanel. She wore five cardigans.

His English had improved by then. We used to eat at a local café. He had never eaten toast with sliced bread before; he loved it. He used to order ten toast please. He also called the Thames the Temiese and he loved malt loaf. In the local supermarket he one day said "'ave you any makelove?" I cried with laughter.

My mother finally agreed but I needed to earn extra money to pay my mum back and to pay for my hotel for a week. Never one to be deterred about life I bought the *Evening Standard*. I looked under the situations vacant part-time work as there were often evening jobs.

There was one that took my fancy, evening sales clerk from 6-8, good remuneration for successful people. I was one of the first cold calling sales brigade we hate so much now. The interview was just by Charing Cross Station in an underground office. It was for The Arthur Murray School of Dance. I was given a page of the current telephone directory and this is what I said:

"Hello my name is Annette from the Arthur Murray School of ballroom dancing. How are you?" Then I would say, "Have you ever tried ballroom dancing?" If they said yes, I would go into the sales blurb about improvement classes, and if they said no I would suggest they come for a free trial with a top instructor who had been on *Come Dancing*, the 1970s version of *Strictly* on a Saturday night.

If you got an appointment you would get an extra three pounds. If you got a show (as they called it) you would get an extra five pounds and if they signed up you would get ten pounds. I am ashamed to say I did very well and saved up quite a bit of money for my ticket and my mum. It was a lot of money in those days.

Off to Corsica – my next chapter.

Chapter Six

So off to Corsica we flew from Heathrow. We paid twenty-two pounds each one-way. It was a white-knuckle flight because of my fear of flying. We landed in Ajaccio, got the bus to the town centre and found a hotel on Cours Napoleon called Hotel Modern, which was not a good description of the place. It was clean with stone floors above the shops. I love the smell of stone houses in hot countries – a very Mediterranean experience.

I fell in love with Corsica in the first week. It smelt lovely and had a different feel about it. It smelt of myrtle and heather. We had breakfast the first morning in a café below the hotel and started our plan of action.

Jean Michel had a map and he pointed out that along the route-des-Sanguinaires there seemed to be a lot of hotels. It was a road which lead to the Iles des Sanguinaires which translated is the island of blood. We bought food for lunch and headed towards the route. It was stunning. It was a winding wild coastline very like Cornwall in places. It went on for miles. So we put our finger out and started to hitch. We got a lift very quickly and they dropped us halfway along.

The hotels started to appear. The first hotel we approached was called Cala de Sole and Jean Michel was offered a job. There was no place for me. He accepted and agreed to start the next Monday when our hotel booking had finished.

We carried on and sat on the next beach and had our lunch. I began to feel very nervous as I had no job. I was English with no French. But we carried on and hitched to the next hotel which was a big hotel set on the opposite of the road to the coastline It was called Hotel des Calangues. We wandered in. There was a big reception area and there was a nice German girl who spoke fluent English. I asked her if there was any work. "Can you speak French as we are looking for receptionists?" she answered.

"No, better at Italian very little French," I told her. She looked disappointed.

She then told me, "The only other thing we have is a chambermaid job. Would you be interested?"

She told me the pay, which was very good for a live-in job, and when I said yes she called the head of housekeeping. Her name was Madam Munroe. She was a short, grey, formidable French woman who asked me a few questions in French which I could just about answer and took me on. I think they were very keen to take on staff because the season was starting. There was no application form to fill in.

So we both started on the Monday in our separate places. My French was next to nothing. I was given a room, it was again with an en suite and put on chambermaid duties. I was on the second level corridor with Annie a French lady who had been doing seasons most of her working life. She did the skiing season in Megeve in winter and Corsica every summer, even though it sounded exciting, she had no boyfriend and no friends to speak of, it felt to me she had got into a rut because she seemed to have no life apart from work. Anyway my French was poor and she had no English at all.

Unbeknown to me Jean Michel had taught me swear words, so I was swearing away in French unknowingly. Annie and I had a trolley for work, and were assigned one of the long corridors on the second floor. We had to finish at the latest at three for new clients to check in. Making the beds was easy for her to explain, but other things were more difficult. My cleaning skills consisted of a bit of hoovering on a Saturday for my mum and a bit of housework in Italy. I did not know how to clean a hotel room properly. Annie shouted at me constantly in French. This is how I learnt very quickly.

One day she shouted, "Lave le vit" which was slang for wash the windows. I just stood there trying to work out what she was saying and she repeated it irritable fashion. Now in school I learnt that the windows in French was most definitely fenetres.

So I stood there getting more and more confused. Eventually. Annie showed me. I pointed at the window and said, "Fenetre," and she pointed to the glass and said, "Vit." So I started learning French slang. That day was a learning day because when we all got together after doing our corridors at three p.m. Madam Monroe shouted, "CA VA?" (You OK?)

"Oui," I replied. And then I went on to say, "Putain bordell de murde le chamber sans degulas aujour hui," (translated fu…g he… the rooms were disgusting today).

Everyone went silent then Madam Munro broke it and said, "Mon dieu les gros mot." (Oh my god swear words.)

She sat me down on a chair held my hand and said, "Annette, sai pas bien ce'st les gros mot." I understood 'pas bien' as Annie had used it most of the day when I did the wrong thing, but 'gros mot' I could not understand. So she called the German girl from the reception who spoke English who explained to me. I apologised and laughed hysterically with her and so did all the French as they realised I did not have a clue what I was saying.

"I am so sorry." I professed to the team I had been swearing at everyone thinking it was good French. They forgave me and all kissed me.

I liked learning to clean the rooms properly. Annie was a perfectionist and it held me in good stead when I opened my own B&B later on in life. At the end of the first week she started saying, "Aujourd'hui chambre blanc," (white room).

I had learnt to say, "Qu'est-ce que c'est," (what is that). She also used the word 'regard' (look) which showed me what to do for a chambre blanc. It means 'change over for new clients' and it translates to white room. So I learnt to do a deep clean. My French improved rapidly and I loved it there because at three o'clock we all went to the beach opposite and played games, swam and had fun wave jumping. The camaraderie was amazing: everyone, chefs, waiters, receptionists, it was great. Not like Italy where I had no time of my own. Jean Michel used to join us. We used to go out clubbing in Ajaccio. It was like a six-month holiday.

One day I was called to reception and the German girl said, "Which is your day off this week?"

I told her, "I do not know as the rota was not done yet. Why?"

She explained. "Well I do the tour for the P&O cruises on Saturdays. We take them on a tour into the mountains to see Napoleon's village. They make a stop for lunch, it's good pay and you get tips. I will talk with Madam Monroe to get you a day off."

So that Saturday I was given a sheet of instructions and was driven to central Ajaccio to meet the P&O ferry. The plan was to put half the tour on the train and the other half on the coach. I was to go on the coach after I put them on the train and then descend with the ones who had mounted on the coach.

So they descended from the boat and I greeted them and then counted them into two halves and told one half to wait there. I took the other half in search of a station. I assumed it was in the centre of Ajaccio just like England. Nobody had told me. So off I went with a crowd of aged middle-class English people looking for a station. After twenty minutes there was one man who was a know all. He realised I did not know where I was going, he spoke fluent French and asked one of the passing French people, "Ou a la station?" (Where is the station?)

He answered, "Il n'existe aucune station, passer les trains du port." (There is no station, the trains go from the port.)

I wanted to die. I had a very angry crowd, so we walked back down to the port and there it was: a train just in front of the P&O ferry. I tried to explain it was my first time and I had not noticed the track at the port and nobody had chosen to tell me. So I put one half on the train and got on the coach with the other half. I was so nervous as I had to read a sheet of history to them on the mike. Not a great thing for a dyslexic. I had never spoken to the public before in my life. I read them some potted history from my sheet about Napoleon growing up in the village and picking oranges in the mountains.

There was another clever clogs on the coach who corrected some of my information. I explained that I merely had been given the sheet and I was not a historian. We stopped halfway up in a typical Corsican bar where they were given eau de vie, a very strong liquor which mellowed them a bit. I suggested a singsong that went down like a lead balloon. My French was pretty good by then and the coach driver was really funny. He said in French quietly, "These are a miserable lot." I explained how they had to wait as I had taken the other half through the town looking for the station, he was crying with laughter.

We stopped in the Napoleon village where the train stopped, had lunch and then put the coach lot on the train and the train lot on the coach. I loved it in the mountains; they were lush with green myrtle and heather. They call the mountain forest, the maquis, which is a shrubbery blanketing more than half the island which produces a fragrance that wafts far out to sea and has earned Corsica its appellation as 'the Scented Isle'. For centuries, the wild maquis provided hideouts for bandits, and the province's history is rich with adventure and mystery. Corsica it is the main symbol of the island. All of the train group were disgruntled. I was not looking forward to the descent. I read through from the sheet again, they were not impressed.

Then my coach driver said, "Tell them a joke."

I said, "I do not know any."

"I do," he said. "Tell them the one about Napoleon's uncle." He then proceeded to tell me, which I translated to the coach members.

"Napoleon's uncle worked in the graveyard and was the laziest man in the village. Napoleon got very angry with his uncle one day and said why was he always lying down on the graves? Why do you not work? Well said the uncle if all these buggers are resting in peace why can't I?"

Suffice to say I did not get a laugh. It went from bad to worse as the coach driver stopped at a garden centre, ran out the coach and bought something for his wife. The party were saying why have we stopped here? I explained I did not have a clue it was down to the coach driver. He then, on the way into Ajaccio stopped at a block of apartments and delivered the thing he had bought at the garden centre. I nearly had a mutiny. To be fair the coach driver's actions were not my fault. I was to learn the Corsicans do what the hell they want. He told me Pasquale Paoli was their true hero not Napoleon, and that he died in England as a friend of King George III. I told them this, even the clever clogs had not heard of him. So I research him when I got back.

Pasquale Paoli switched allegiance during the French Revolution. He had been exiled by the monarchy, he was an idol for liberty and democracy. He was a good man and was not happy with the king being executed. Then he was accused of treason. He asked the British government for protection who were at war in France. He suggested that Corsica might be like another Ireland to Britain. Britain sent a fleet in 1794. It was the battle where Nelson lost his sight in one eye. For a very short time Britain ruled Corsica under King George III.

The relationship between Paoli's government and the King's representative, Sir Gilbert Elliot, and Paoli's republican leanings and desire to defend Corsican autonomy was very difficult, so the British decided to retreat. And Paoli had no choice than to retreat with the British. The French took back Bastia in 1796.

In 1807 a monument to this famous Corsican was erected in the south choir aisle of Westminster Abbey. It is of white marble and includes a bust of Paoli which had been made some years earlier by the sculptor, John Flaxman. The inscription reads:

'D.O.M. To the memory of Pasquale De Paoli, one of the most eminent and most illustrious characters of the age in which he lived. He was born at Rostino, in Corsica, April 5th 1725, was unanimously chosen, at the age of thirty supreme head of that island, and died in this metropolis February 5th 1807, aged eighty-two years. In the early and better part of his life he devoted to the cause of liberty; nobly maintaining it against the usurpation of Genoese and French tyranny: by his many splendid achievements, his useful and benevolent institutions, his patriotic and public zeal manifested upon every occasion, he, amongst the few who have merited so glorious a title, most justly deserved to be hailed the Father of his country. Being obliged by the superior forces of his enemies to retire from Corsica, he sought refuge in this land of liberty; and was here most graciously received (amidst the general applause of a magnanimous nation) into the protection of his Majesty King George III: by whose fostering hand and munificence, he not only obtained a safe and honourable asylum, but was enabled during the remainder of his days, to enjoy the society of his friends and faithful followers, in affluent and dignified retirement. He expressed to the last moment of his life the most grateful sense of His Majesty's paternal goodness towards him, praying for the preservation of his sacred person, and the prosperity of his dominions.'

Some of the party said that they were going to complain to P&O, as this is disgusting. Finally I got back to the port. I was relieved it was over. A couple of nice people who thought the whole thing hysterical gave me big tips and told me not to worry. I never did another guided tour. But I was very interested in Pasquale as he had died in England.

I was glad to get back to the safety of chamber-maiding. Annie was much more manageable than a crowd of pompous middle-class English tourists who did not care about Paoli Pasquale, my newfound hero.

I enjoyed my season in Corsica. I had so much fun. I saved up £1000. Mostly because I had tips and lived off them and did not touch our wages. We did not find Jean Michel's family although we did a lot of research how to get there but the train took too long in those days, as his family were based in the mountains in the north of the island around Bastia. That was the other side of the island.

One morning there was a commotion at breakfast as the bank that the hotel used, where all our wages were, was bombed by Corsican separatists. At three o'clock there was a mass exodus to Ajaccio to see what had happened. We arrived and were assured our money was OK and the bank down the road was holding our money now. Great relief for all.

Mid-season two more English people came to work at the hotel: Heather and Pete. They were from Yorkshire. They were slightly hippy and really lovely. The French could not say Heather as they could not pronounce the H. They called her les oeufs so that was a constant joke as it meant the eggs. When any one said, "Ou est les œufs," (where is Heather), they would all shout, "Dans les fridgadaire." (In the fridge)

They were at breakfast that morning, so I asked them, "What are Corsican separatists?" They explained they are like the IRA, they want an independent Corsica. Jean Michel also explained later that his family were true Corsicans and in the area of Corsican Nationals. I loved the Corsicans they are passionate and I feel Corsica is my second home. They have saved it from invasion of the English and have preserved it. To love one's island like they do is special, although I do not condone violence.

I had a great time with Heather and Pete. We used to go clubbing although it was called discoing then, we often walked back along the Route des Sanguinaires. One particular night we were teaching the French and Corsicans, 'On Ilkla Moor Baht At'.

It was so funny hearing them trying to sing in a Yorkshire accent. Heather and Pete were travelling through like our gap years now and decided to go to Sardinia. They said why do you not come with us. I was really tempted and spoke to Jean Michel. He went mad and screamed. He had become very possessive and insecure about me. He persuaded me not to go and I finished the season in Corsica.

I also had an Arabic friend called Sala. He was jolly. He was saving up for his wife and children to build a house in Morocco, he sent all his money back. But he wanted to speak English. I was very naughty. I taught him 'I am a crazy fool'. He used to say, "I am crazen fool." He taught me equally as bad in Arabic. 'Abba asma nich bah vic', I do not know what it means to this day. But the Arabs used to fall around laughing. I taught him some good English. He was a loving family man who always had a smile for everyone. He used to vacuum all the corridors.

We used to go to the cinema in Ajaccio occasionally and there was a buzz around the hotel one day. It was the film *L'histoire du O* (The Story of O). It was a very sexy film. We all went en-mass. I was shocked because there was every age at the showing; kids running around and elderly people, unlike England. The best film I saw was *A Nous Les Petites Anglaises.* It was about a French school trip to Ramsgate, it was great. Placed during the fifties the group ended up at a local dance. In one of the scenes the French boys put soda bottles down the trousers and danced with the English girls. Consequently the English girls thought all French boys were well endowed. It was so funny.

We returned to England. I cried. I did not want to leave Corsica. I had fallen in love with it: the beautiful mountains, the beaches and its haunting aura. There was no work in the winter when we left. It was slightly more successful than my Italian trip and I visited Jean Michel's grandmother in Solesmes, North France near Cambrai.

She was a formidable lady who Jean Michel called Mammie. She was in her seventies, not a grey hair on her head. Every night before bed she would eat raw garlic on buttered French bread. She claimed she had never had a cold or flu in her life. Jean Michel joined her. We were in a bateau bed with a sloping mattress, which sank into the middle and he stank, it was so strong. She had a lovely house in Solesmes and a house near Paris. He husband had been a successful builder. His brother Jean Yves had been bought up by Mammie and still lived with her. Jean Michel was eager to see him again. He was becoming more possessive. He would not let me pack my own suitcase.

At the end of the season in Corsica he had insisted I bought decent French clothes with a name, so we bought a Ted Lapidus camelhair coat. It was a waisted, fifties style, a pair of very expensive leather boots and some other clothes with names. Now I am not the least interested in names, never have been, never will. So the arguments were horrific. It got to the stage where he would pack my case and not let me take anything from it because I was untidy. We argued a lot. He was extremely insecure and looking back he fell in love with me, and I with him. I was the first person who ever showed him love and he was going to do what he thought to protect it. He started to suffocate me. But I still loved him. His brother returned to England with us and my mum let them stay with us. Jimmy, my brother, became great friends with Jean Yves.

Jimmy had a garage band with his friends: Dave, Ian, Ziggy, Makay, Kirk, Russell, Lee and Jed. We all used to and hang around there, Jim wrote a song called 'Garage Band Blues' which I always loved. Jean Michel played guitar in a classical style and I played nothing and could not sing. I have always loved music. My daughter is an extremely good musician: piano, violin, flute, voice and guitar. I finally did a New Year's resolution about three years ago to learn violin and now I can play. I love it. I can actually read music. I stepped over a fear. I thought never in a million years could I, a dyslexic, read music but I can. It is in fact easy for a dyslexic as it is symbols with no word formation.

Jean Michel, Jean Yves and I went to Megeve to do the skiing season – it was lovely. I got a job looking after a child for a while. But Jean Yves and Jean Michel failed to get jobs. I think they were catching up. I was a bit annoyed as I was working and paying for everything. I nearly hit Jean Yves one day, when I asked him if he got the job he went for. He was in a café with a group of Brittany guys. "No!" he said.

I said, "Why not?"

He said, "The head chef said 'can you do fish?' (His answer was to open and closed his mouth feigning to be a fish.) The chef had no sense of humour. I was so angry.

I changed my job to chambermaiding because it was more money and I worked with a couple who were *pied noir.* I did not know what that meant. I thought it was people with black feet. But it is repatriated French from Africa. They were a brother and sister, very tall with dark hair, strange looking.

I had the last bedroom on the top floor, and after working there for a few weeks I heard a knock on my door about eleven p.m. I was asleep but I woke up. It was the brother. He was drunk and tried to get in my room. I pushed the door against his foot and screamed, luckily his sister heard, came running and took him away. I ran to where Jean Michel was staying and he came back and shouted at him. The sister calmed it all down. He apologised and said it would never happen again, he was drunk. Saying that I would lie in bed at nights worried about him returning, I wanted to go home to England. This experience had marred the season.

My mum always phoned where I was and when she heard she insisted I returned. "I will send the money."

"I do not want to owe you," I cried.

"I will transfer it to a bank." That's what you had to do in those days. Jean Michel would go daily to the bank and see if it had arrived. Then one day he came and said he had found some money.

I said, "Where?"

"In a church," he said. "We can all go back to England." I was so relieved I did not question it any more. I think he did it because he was worried about me in the hotel.

But on the plane home he told me he took it from the bank. He was in the manager's office and it was lying on the desk when the manager has left to see if my mum's money had a telex in.

I was so angry and worried, then halfway through the flight he looked at me and said you are only smiling one side of your face. I looked in the mirror in the toilet. He was right, I was paralysed on one side of my face. The shock and stress of everything had given me Bell's palsy. Things got worse when we arrived at Heathrow. Jean Michel was arrested, not for stealing the money, but as an IRA suspect. I tried to convince the police he was French. But they showed me a photo of an identical Irish man and they thought he was cleverly putting on a French accent. My mum arrived at Heathrow, finally vouched for him and they let him go. It was because he had grown a beard in Megeve.

The French bank had phoned my mother and she had agreed to pay the money back. It was slightly more than she had telexed over. She shouted at them both and told them to go and get jobs. I went to the doctors who told me to rest and take the medicine he gave me or I could be stuck with one side of my face not working for life. Luckily with rest after two weeks my face started working again.

Jean Michel and Jean Yves got a job in the St James's Gentleman's Club Piccadilly with all the old peers. I started temping again.

Chapter Seven

Marriage in Pruno

I was back to England in 1970, I decided to temp. I went and signed on to Alfred Marks and Reid. Jean Michel got a job in The St James's Club, a gentleman's club in Piccadilly.

I got a job as a telephonist, I had never worked a switchboard before, but my mum had worked them all. So a lady who ran the temps in Alfred Marks said, "Can you work a doll's eye switchboard I am desperate, do you think you could wing it?" She let me phone my mum who said she would talk me through it in the morning when I arrived at the job. Ironically it was an accountants in Old Burlington Street opposite IFW. I arrived in the morning and called my mum and she talked me through the doll's eye. There were two rows of plastic type eyeballs which clicked up and down when the lines were being used. There were also holes underneath and a row of connecting plugs for different extensions. One row for incoming calls and the other row for extensions, so you would plug the corresponding two plugs together in order for the two parties to communicate. You also had headphones. You are expecting disaster but no my mum talked me through. I only cut off two people and blamed the exchange and there I was another string to my dyslexic bow – a telephonist.

I temped around London, in the City and West End, all sorts of companies, sometimes as a receptionist, which was the most boring job on earth. I would have to stamp the post with a franking machine. I used to dream about having my own business one day where it would be my post.

By now in 1974 I had lots of different skills: sales, telephonist, telex, typing, photocopying, clean a hotel room to a chambre blanc standard, French, some Italian. My skills were growing. I was fascinated by business and how people started them. I wanted to work for me eventually.

The following year I returned to Corsica for a second season in a different hotel where Jean Michel and I worked in the same hotel. This time I did bar, reception and waitressing.

On the 22nd July 1976 it was Jean Michel's birthday. We went out for a lovely meal we always ate the same soup: du poisson and for dessert: soufflé pour deux.

All the staff had rooms in an annex of the hotel. We got back, made love and shortly after going to sleep we both woke up with a start. There was a ghostly woman standing at the bottom of our bed. She looked like an angel and then she disappeared. I shouted, "Did you see that?" I had shouted so loud it woke all the other staff up.

Jean Michel was lying there with a dazed shocked look, and said, "Yes I did," very slowly. We held on to each other, frightened. The other staff were knocking on the door shouting 'what has happened?' We told them and they were all terrified. None of us went to sleep that night. The owner of the hotel started questioning me about it because someone had told her about the incident. But for some reason in my heart I knew I was not to tell her, don't ask me why. I asked Jean Michel recently if he remembers what happened. He said he did very clearly.

That night I fell pregnant even thought I was on the on the pill then and had been for a long time and I gave birth to my beautiful daughter Angelique on 10th April 1977.

We tried to make it work but Jean Michel had OCD. His life had been very difficult. He did not see his mother after his dad had taken him from her and the island. His father was a director of a mental hospital and they lived on site in Paris. His father also married seven times and none of the wives were nice to Jean Michel. They were Parisian socialites. He was left to his own devices and had little to no nurturing. I did not know this when we met. I also had serious childhood issues, losing two fathers, so our relationship did not have a chance.

He was so obsessive if you moved a cotton wool bud from his pot, even if it was half full, he would know. He was getting more and more possessive and controlling. I could not cope so I asked him to leave the flat we had. I understand what happened in retrospect but as young people we did not take into consideration our backgrounds and our lack of nurturing. We were looking to each other for nurturing which is on some level normal in a relationship, but when backgrounds are that unstable neither can facilitate the other. Also as my best friend Jan used to say I was wild and free and she was more constrained, that works with a friend but with a relationship it is a disaster.

Fast Forward.

Bath early 2000s.

By now I am with Adrian. Jean Michel is living in the Alps with Josian and their son Micele. Angelique has seen him in

France over the years. He had often talked about finding his Corsican family.

I have been with Adrian for several years and promised to take him to Corsica. I booked a holiday in the north of the island, Cap Corse. I wanted to see it as I missed going in the 1970s

Angelique is grown up and living with her childhood sweetheart.

Before I went on holiday, "Guys," she said thoughtfully over a cup of tea to Adrian and I, "if you are going to Corsica could you look for Dad's family? I know he would love to find them."

So off we went on holiday to Cap Corse, the search took over our holiday. We booked in with an English woman who was married to a Corsican. She upgraded us on the second night to her apartment by the sea: it was lovely. It overlooked a typical Genoese tower, which dated back to the fifteenth century. They were built to stop the Ottoman Turks invading and capturing the Corsicans and selling them as slaves. They line the coastline. They're round with a roof terrace for look outs. There were a hundred built. They are often seen in the advertising brochures of Cap Corse. We sat out and watched the sea at dusk with a glass of Corsican wine, contemplating our mission. Adrian loves my children, Angelique and Dominic like his own, as I do his daughter Alice. He would do anything to make them happy. He embraced the mission with all his heart.

We asked the lady from the bed and breakfast, how we could find my ex-husbands family, she said I should go to the main Marie in Bastia and ask do you have names. I had Jean Michel's date of birth. So after some fun on the beach we ventured into central Bastia. We found the Marie and I was treated with the utmost respect. I think it was because I had actually married a

Corsican and had had a child. He found Jean Michel's birth certificate and there it was the names and addresses of his parents: Felicity Albertini and Micelle Martin.

His mother's village was named, Loreto-di-Casinca. We asked the clerk where it was, who said it was way up in the mountains high. He said it is true Corsica. You take the road to the south and you will find a sign at the sixth roundabout you go all the way up. Adrian said, "Let's go now," so I agreed. Off we went. We found the roundabout and went up through one village then up to another and another. We kept driving up. I felt a bit sick with the constant turning. Finally we arrived in the square of the mountain village. We parked in the square and looked around. In front of us was the Marie, it was a typical Marie building, but to the left there were two wooden doors which were opened to reveal carcasses, sausages and hanging salami. I was going to learn about the wild boar later and to the left on the other side was a bar. Adrian said, "Let's go in the bar and ask." We walked through the door and there were locals chatting. They all looked up and went silent, you could hear a pin drop. They continued to say nothing and stared, we both felt nervous. I ordered a drink and we sat down. Adrian pushed me and said go and show the bar man the birth certificate and ask him if he knows them. I gingerly went back to the bar, all eyes on me and showed him. He said, "Yes," and in a strong accent he said go to the Marie. I went back to the table and told Adrian. He said, "Go to the Marie, go on then," Adrian encouraged me.

"Are you all right here?" I asked.

"Yes I will read my book."

I walked nervously across the square and went down a long alley, then up the stairs to room that said Marie. I knocked and a woman opened the door. She was lovely. I showed her the birth certificate. "Ah," she said. "It is the cousin of the mayor. I will call him." A very burly mayor came rushing in and said it was his cousin but Felicity lived in Lyon in France now, so I gave him my telephone number and ask him to pass it on to her.

Upon returning to the bar a little disappointed, Adrian looked up from his book and said, "How did it go?"

Then the barman started madly gesticulating to me. "Come with me," he insisted.

I looked at Adrian. "Should I go?"

"Yes," he said, "go." We just went round the corner. He knocked on the door of a house and he said, "Frere?" which means brother. I explained to the man at the door who I was. He invited me in. I said I had Adrian with me and went and got him.

It was a typical mountain house. He told us his name was Charlot. It was lovely, they got out the eau de vie and told me the names of all his brothers and sisters. Showed us photos it was amazing. He proudly showed us his vegetable patch. He lived with a woman called Mimie and he called his sister Angele who lived in a mountain village called Pruno nearby. She was so excited and wanted to meet us. We had arranged to go south the next day, as I wanted to return to Ajaccio and see Boniface. So we made an arrangement to meet the day after. Charlot then took us to his garage and showed us his pride and joy: a sparkling old Volvo with a satnav. I asked him why he needed a satnav, he explained he had lived in Marseilles for most of his life and retired here.

I called Angelique, she was so excited. We had a lovely day and night down south. I showed Adrian where I had worked. Jean Michel's hotel was still operating but mine was derelict and then we drove towards our rendezvous with Angele. We had arranged to meet Paul, Angele's husband, in a café in Forrelli which was right on the road from the south which we were on. When we arrived Paul came out of the bar and shook our hands. His French was hard to understand as he has beautiful Corsican accent and he said to follow him. He got in his van and drove up to the mountain. On the way up he stopped at a vegetable garden, which we now always call 'Le garden du Paul's', and he picked up an axe. We were a bit spooked but we continued to follow. Then all of a sudden there was a village parked on the side of the hill – it was stunning. We drove through the archway to the village and then down a steep incline to Angele and Paul's house.

It was an instant rapport with Angele. She is wonderful. We were invited in. They fed us with the beautiful food which comes from the garden of Paul and the boars they shoot. Every now and then they would shout at each other in Corsican, we are used to it now. But then we did not know what was going on as they spoke Corsican not French. I would ask Angele on subsequent visits after, what was said. It was minor like, why did you not get the milk out? Angele told us all about Felicity and we got Angelique on the phone. The view from the patio is amazing. It is literally overhanging the mountain with a view to die for. The homemade wine and everything, the ambiance was magical. I thought if only we had come in the seventies. Their cellar looks like a store for a high class deli, but it is all of the produce Angele and Paul had lovingly grown, pickled and salted. I love the simplicity of it.

It was a success. I told Angele I did stained glass. She said excitedly that she wanted a window for the church. She was in charge of the church, and had the keys, the window was just squares and very dilapidated. The church was beautiful and

Angele showed me a statue which she had raised money for. Angele is a formidable woman. Both Angelique and myself love Angele. She asked me to get a price for the window and to do a design. Charlot and Meme invited us back to Loreto for a meal which we accepted. That was a wonderful experience as it was in an even more dramatic than Angele's and Paul's balcony. It was the old church on the edge of a cliff which was now a restaurant with a view right out to sea. It was lovely. Charlot has now passed which is sad as we had a fantastic meal and bon Amie with him and Meme that night.

Angelique visited many times as we did. Her father now lives in Corsica near the family. Angelique fell in love with Pruno and wanted to get married there – Angele's village. I had chosen the name Angelique. Jean Michel wanted an English name. I fought for it and unbeknown Angele existed.

So we arranged the wedding in Corsica. It was on April 10th, Angelique's birthday, and I had also sorted the design for the church window. On the previous visit we had taken Angele a Maquette (a small sample of a stained glass window design), which she approved with Christophe, the priest, and the village. So Adrian and I prepared everything for our next trip. We decided to install the window in time for the wedding. We also had to arrange the wedding from England. We took our own hand blown Bath Aqua glasses from my glass company I know own (which Steve, my future son-in-law, had blown) for the table. Dyliss, Angelique's future mother-in-law, is a great seamstress and did tablecloths and organised the food.

Adrian and I drove down with all that we could fit in for the wedding a week before the wedding with the stained-glass window. The design for the window was Mary the night before the birth of Jesus backed with a Corsican landscape. I brought the Corsican feel to it and I am very pleased with it. The Corsican life is a slower pace than ours. I asked them to have the scaffolding up on our arrival so we could get the window in before the wedding, we had a week. We arrived three days before Leekie, my pet name for Angelique. When we arrived, it was wonderful we arrived to a pile of peas on the kitchen table – it was huge. We spent the evening shelling peas, drinking and eating. I asked about the scaffolding and they told me not to worry. By the third day I got worried. Leekie and Steve arrived and Paul suggested he took Steve to get the scaffolding. Steve explained his experience. He could not speak English. Paul just talks anyway in Corsican. He drives very quickly around the mountain as he is used to it. He terrified Steve picking up bits of scaffolding from verges. Not knowing Steve I think Paul thought he was a soft city slicker. But Steve is very capable. Paul put the scaffolding up with some of his compatriots. Steve was going to help Adrian take the old window out. When he looked up at the scaffolding then suddenly Steve burst out with, "I am fucking getting married in a few days I am not going up there. It looks like a Heath Robinson construction, what about health and safety?" He had a point and is very conscious of health and safety, so it was down to me and Adrian and the stonemason of the village. The old window came out relatively easily and we had to dig out the frame and take out all the masonry.

For the wedding reception we had agreed to use the village hall just up from the Marie. It is a relatively modern building compared to the others in the village, When we first showed it to Steve he was in shock. It was grimy, un-loved and he could not see our vision. He looked stressed and depressed but when we started cleaning it, the vision was gradually coming to him as the view from the windows is magnificent. The hall came alive. We covered the chairs with cloth and ribbon and we put up curtains with matching ribbons, it transformed the building Steve started to see our vision. We had aqua ribbons on the chairs, matching aqua serviettes. With our Bath Aqua glasses sparkling and all Dyliss's wonderful work it looked magnificent.

We had aqua coloured favours and table names. Before I left England a friend said to me you need to be careful in Corsica the whole village usually turns up. I had asked Angele to have all the names for the table because Dyliss and I were worried about the catering. Dyliss did a great job. She did true English dishes: Coronation chicken and other English delicacies. The Corsicans provided wild boar produce and salads from Le Garden du Paul. Paul insisted on loads and loads of French sticks. I told him that we did not eat the bread like them. Dyliss had made a fabulous cake. We had agreed to have the two traditions combined and had an agreed schedule.

Angelique had arranged the services so we were almost ready. The window was well on its way. We had to make a template for the top of the window so it would fit and I finished the rounded top part of the window in the church which was a success. After a lot of screaming by both us and the Corsicans we got the window in. The lovely older lady with a window facing the church made my day. She lent out and said, "I am so happy, the virgin Mary smiles at me every time I look out of the window." It had cheered her up no end. I was delighted.

Arrangements were coming together, then Angelique said you must tell Angele to cancel the disco. I said why. She said Paul's nephew Thierry has offered to do the music for free. Now

Thierry bless him is severely Asperger's and you could see he was not quite right, but Leekie insisted. I told Angele who just looked at me in total shock. But she did not say anything and agreed to cancel the disco. Jean Yves, Leekie's uncle, arrived in the village the next day. He said, "I have something to tell you, Annette, you have upset the Corsicans."

I was shocked. "Why?" I said.

He said, "You cancelled the disco which has been arranged for months."

I said, "Angelique told me Thierry is doing the music."

He laughed. "What the fuck he is going to do it with his mobile phone? He is special, haven't you noticed?"

I told him, "I have but Leekie insisted." I cried with laughter. I thought Leeks had worked it out with him and he had equipment. Angelique was practising her music with her friends in the church. I couldn't stop laughing and was bent over.

She looked at me. "What on earth's the matter?" I couldn't speak through laughter. I could see in my mind's eye Thierry at the wedding with his mobile phone playing the music. Jean Yves followed me and, after he had kissed and greeted her, he told her what he told me. She then was bent over laughing. She couldn't believe I had thought he could do it. "Mum, can you tell him he is not doing it and fix it with Angele?" she said. Of course I did. Angele also cried with laughter when I finally told her. Thierry got really stroppy when I told him and said he would not come to the wedding. My stress levels were rising. We had forty English guests coming. They were all staying at Grace's B&B and caravans at the bottom of the mountain. I asked Angele once again if the whole village would turn up. She assured me no.

The stonemason, Adrian and I worked tirelessly to get the window finished.

Then Paul told us of a local marriage tradition and offered to make a beautiful garland to arch the door of the church, so he took Adrian and showed him how to make a wild garland. It was beautiful. Adrian really enjoyed the experience and made one for us when we got married.

Angele placed flowers in the church and at the end of the pews, it looked beautiful. The Virgin Mary window was installed, looking down on my beautiful daughter getting married. Who would have thought I would have designed this window in the church my daughter got married in.

I had a sudden thought and wondered then if it had all meant to be as we saw the vision the night Angelique was conceived.

Corsican weddings are different to English weddings so we took a bit of time to agree what was what. The first official stage of the wedding was to be at the Marie and a walk up to the church for the service. It is tradition in Corsica that everyone walks in a line from the bride's house together. First it was Angelique with her Uncle Jean Yves and her brother Dominic who gave her away, then the bridesmaids, then Steve with his best men Stuart and Steve Saxty, then Dyliss and Adrian and myself and Steve's dad Phil. Then the rest followed. I loved it – it was like a procession.

My best friend Tammy and her husband and son were there. And just before the procession I only had two minutes to get ready, as I had been making the canapes. Tammy helped me dress and threw make-up on me. "Oh my god, do I look all right?" I said.

"Don't worry about that you look lovely," she assured me. So we ventured into the front room Angelique was being photographed on the balcony, she looked so fabulous she really looked like a top model. Dyliss had made the bridesmaids' dresses. I was really surprised when I saw the Corsicans outside: they were all in black. I learned that is their tradition. It was an amazing contrast with the English as we were in bright colours. I think they were shocked at our regalia. We took our places. I walked with Steve's dad. We held hands, it was very touching.

We arrived at the Marie and the Mayor did the vows. He made a wonderful speech about Pasquale Paoli and the connection with L'Angleterre. We then walked to the church and the service began. My daughter looked so happy. She had created a musical extravaganza with her choir. Steve's sister Debbie sang a solo. After the vows there was silence. Angelique got up and took her place next to her music and to our complete surprise burst into the 'Song Bird' by Fleetwood Mac. As soon as she sang 'For you there will be no more crying. For you the sun will be shinning' I lost it. Steve lost it and all the English burst into tears. Steve's shoulders were going up and down. She continued, she sang it perfectly, I was so proud of her. I cannot listen to that song without weeping. Steve Saxty, one of the best men, moved over to Steve and gave him a hug to keep him going. It was one of the most beautiful moments of my life. I had pride, happiness that my daughter had found the love of her life early and had enjoyed him and was now marrying him.

We left the church and outside everyone was happy. Angelique was taken by Paul to the stone veranda of the village and given a shotgun to fire along with five other nationalists. The guns went off. Steve looked around, there was his new wife in a wedding dress shooting with the Corsicans, the noise was loud and we all cheered. The photos are great. I then ran on to the reception to check the canapés Tammy had got up earlier to prepare.

We served the champagne and the canapés, but most of the village did turn up. I thought they were leaving after the pre wedding drinks, but no, so we had to do some jiggery-pokery to fit them in. Adrian was master of ceremonies as he always is. We even had people we did not expect from the campsite and Mr Silvio, the builder who worked for Angele's daughter, Anne Marie. He was one of the best dancers I have ever seen. He was from Brazil.

The next part as agreed was the English way; with our toasts and speeches they were lovely. Steve thanked his mum as she had worked so tirelessly. Dominic made a perfect speech as he had given his sister away. Jean Yves read out a heartfelt message from Jean Michel who could not be there because his wife was ill. Then Adrian did some hip hip hurrahs which the Corsicans loved, so we did about twenty. It was so funny. "hip hip hooray." I looked across the room and there was Thierry, of the disco fame, who had refused to come. He was sitting stuffing his face at a table like a cuckoo. I laughed as he was fine. I went around the tables to chat. Tammy was on the table with German Eric from the campsite. She could hardly speak through laughing. Eric had thought the coronation chicken was a dessert and eaten it with sweet things.

The guy from the disco arrived. I apologised to him and he was OK and the party began to rock. Now we have had many a fine evening singing with the Corsicans on our many visits, they sing from the soul. The wedding was no different. The Corsican on one side of the room sang songs at us. Then we sang 'Swing Low Sweet Chariot' back. They sang one, we sang one. It was fabulous. We danced and I gave Leekie a cuddle. She said, "Mum this has been the best day of my life." That made my night.

Adrian was driving people up and down the hill all day; he is my star. We finally got to bed at three, knackered but happy. Adrian had driven Leeks and Steve to their hotel near the airport. She had lost the name of the hotel, they drove around for ages. She had about an hour in it as they had an early start to catch the plane for their honeymoon.

The next day the rain poured. We cleared up the hall and that was the end of a beautiful wedding. We all had lunch in the hall, chewing over the previous day. It was a lovely finish.

We had a little holiday with Tammy and David and their son in France. We drove down to Bonifacio. In fact I was so tired I fell asleep on the beach with my tummy sticking out and my lovely best friend Tammy took my picture. I was glad she was there at the wedding: she was a great support.

I felt Adrian and I achieved something great in those two weeks. His French had improved immensely and he had fitted that window with tenacity and love. We are a good team but it was not always like that. We had to work at it.

Chapter Eight

Bringing up the Children

By this stage in the 1980's I have two children, Angelique and Dominic. It is life's most important work which I loved. Not being in a supportive relationship I had to do it pretty much on my own? I felt it was a big responsibility. I realised I was bringing up the next generation and I wanted them to have capabilities and an education, so I threw myself into their development. I also as a child was a latch key kid, a child who let themselves in after school, whilst their parents were working. I did not want that for my children. I wanted to be at home after school for them. Which meant finding jobs that I could do in school time, around the children. So here started my jack-of-all-trades and master of none career.

I worked as a cleaner which was well paid and I could organise my times within school times and my clients often let me take the children during the holidays. I did waitressing for a very up market restaurant, Morels, which was great fun. I worked at a spiritual retreat. I did cooking for a health food restaurant and I worked in an estate agency. I bought and sold houses.

Cleaning was hard work but it was good money, if you live in an area with wealthy households they all want a cleaner. I was a good cleaner because I took pride in whatever job I did. So I was in demand. One of my jobs was for an old couple who were expatriates. Their rooms were full of oversized foreign furniture, big carved wooden tables and oversized coffee tables. A lot of Chinese statues and jade ornaments. It was on three floors and they were in their nineties. The first time I cleaned the bath it was black. It looked like Neil from the Young Ones had bathed there. They did not have a clue as their eyesight was bad. It was quite funny. But I bleached it and scrubbed it clean. They were a very lovely couple and I enjoyed my time there.

One of the other jobs I had was in a big rambling house with a younger eccentric Surrey lady who lived in chaos. Her husband worked in the city and the children were away at private school but the house was in complete chaos. She loved me. I used to organise it back into a semblance of order. Although my own house was in chaos, I was often so exhausted cleaning others that my own suffered. It's called a busmen's holiday.

I loved my time at Morels Restaurant as the people I worked with became friends. Morels was run by Jean Yves and Marianne Morel. Jean Yves had trained with Michel Roux in Bray and was a great chef. The restaurant was on the High Pavement in the town of Haslemere where I lived. It was in the eighties and the time of the first nouvelle cuisine. The restaurant was frequented by many celebrities. I served Gerald Scarf and Jane Asher, Terry from Terry and June, among many others. One of my favourite couples was Roger Taylor of Queen and his beautiful French wife, she was lovely. We used to joke about our Anglo-French children. I had Angelique. The restaurant was run very well and was beautifully decorated.

Mrs Morel, who was called Marianne, had a flair for creating a lovely atmosphere, she would play Billy Holiday and the candles and the white table clothes with the stylish glassware created a really classy restaurant. Marianne was also a stylish dresser and always felt in control.

That was the front restaurant, now the kitchen was a different story. That was run by Jean Yves Morrell, a lovely crazy Frenchman. So we as waiters and waitresses were working in two different atmospheres. For example Jean Yves would plate up two beautiful nouvelle cuisine plates. I would go to get them with my white cloth to pick them up, and with his strong French accent he would say, "Please, Annette, do not destroy my work." Then he would pinch you so the sauce would go everywhere. Then he would shout, "And tidy it up, you are ruining my work." You would then have to compose yourself to go out into the world of Marianne at the front restaurant. You would smile deposit the plates and say bon appetite and then go back to kitchen and call him a bastard.

The washer upper was my good friend, Andy, who is Ethiopian. He was so funny and never arrived to work on time. It used to drive Jean Yves mad, but never fazed Andy. Also Jackie, Bernard and Christophe worked with us. Jackie is Scottish and small and reminded me of Lulu. She was from Glasgow. I am still friends with Jackie now. She eventually married Bernard and had three children and lives in France. Bernard was from the same village as Jean Yves in the hills between Grenoble and Lyon. We all became good friends. Andy was an Ethiopian refugee who lived at the Ockenden Venture, a refugee charity, which owned a big old rambling house in Haslemere which housed refugees. Andy was there with his brothers and sister. I only knew him and his sister Sophia, who had one of the most beautiful faces on earth.

One particular service Andy had arrived late and changed the time on the clock so Jean Yves did not know. We were sat down eating our pre-staff meal and customers started walking in. Andy had to confess. Jean Yves did his usual screaming at him, which went straight over Andy's head. Jean Yves really liked Andy and never sacked him, but called him all the names under the sun.

Then Jean Yves found something out about Andy from Miss Grey who ran the Okenden Venture, that Andy was actually a close relative of Haile Selassie. So halfway through the service Jean Yves said, "Annette, Jackie, do you know why Andy is always late?"

"No," we replied in unison intrigued at what Jean Yves was going to say.

"Well our washer upper is not a common old washer upper. He is related to Haile Selassie, born in Ethiopia in 1892, who was crowned emperor in 1930 but exiled during World War II after leading the resistance to the Italian invasion. He was reinstated in 1941 and sought to modernize the country over the next few decades through social, economic and educational reforms. He ruled until 1974, when famine, unemployment and political opposition forced him from office. The leader of Ethiopia." He had obviously looked it up.

So Jean Yves continued, "Andy is not used to working." Andy did his usual 'Oh Jean Yves' after we called him Prince Andy. Andy was one of the loveliest people I ever met. He had had to leave Ethiopia because of grave danger to his family connections. To be quite honest he did not talk about it much.

I loved jumble sales and they were brilliant in Haslemere, you never had to buy anything new. I kept my kids and myself clothed. So Andy and I decided to do car boot sales. Andy had quite a big car and he would arrive and I would have everything in suitcases and load up his car. We used to joke that the neighbours would think I was running away with him. Suffice to say the car boot sales were not terribly successful and, after we had loaded up at the end of the car boot, Andy would always drive off just as I was about to get in the car. I would be running after it up the road. After that I got a job at the Haslemere hospital in the kitchen and then the Ethiopian crisis set in. Andy was very upset to see his country suffering so much, so we organised (long before Bob Geldof) a sale and raised some money to send to the Ethiopian funds.

Andy turned up in Bath about two years ago. He walked into my shop. He had been down to see me several times but not for years. He looked at me and said, "I have a friend who works here." He did not recognize me.

I said, "Andy it is me." He told me he was now back in Ethiopia but he and his family had returned from Ethiopia because his beautiful sister Sophia had passed away. She had stayed in London. He was with his beautiful family. Both Adrian and I had coffee with them all, it was so lovely to see him.

I'd had enough of cleaning and had done some cooking for a health food shop with a very good friend Eleanor and bought the local paper. There was a very interesting job, working in a spiritual retreat in Waggoners Wells near Headley Down about six miles from Haslemere. So I answered the advert for a cook. I was very good at vegetarian cooking and catering for special diets, as I had my own allergies. So off I went for an interview.

When I arrived it was a lovely house in beautiful grounds. I met with Eddie Burks who had a voice just like Max Bygraves, a gruff gentle cockney sound, with a very soothing presence. His colleague, Jill, was with him. They explained it was a spiritual retreat for anyone who needed their help. The interview went well and I started the next Monday. It was wonderful. I took all my cook books down and for the first time ever I had a budget to buy decent food, to feed the visitors who came for spiritual help and recuperation. My best friend Tammy always said, "You brought your children up on fresh air and lentils." I do not want to be negative about anyone but it is a fact of life that Dominic's dad, my partner, drank too much. So money was very thin on the ground. But he gave me the biggest gift on earth, managing on nothing. My kids joke about my burnt lentil surprise. It is a great dish but being dyslexic I was always preoccupied whilst cooking and sometimes let it burn on the bottom. I used stinging nettles to substitute spinach. I had a friendly grocer, Ted, who let me have stewing veg cheap. You can always make a stew if you put garlic and chilli in it; it lasts for days. The gift my alcoholic partner gave me was cash flowing which transferred into business acumen. I went into see Ted one day. He was a dead ringer for Benny Hill and always had a tale to tell, we would always end up laughing. He had had a party once and not many had turned up. This had irked him. He said that he had a great business idea: bowls of fruit on the coffin instead of flowers. "Do think it will catch on, Annette?"

The vision came into my head. "Would people eat the fruit or would they put it on the grave?"

"Eat it of course," he replied.

"Oh." I said. "Do you think they would want to eat fruit off a coffin. Well that's a no goer."

"I have had another idea," he said excitedly. "No bugger came to my party so if I pretend to have a funeral I bet they will come. I could lie in the coffin with a bowl of fruit on it and surprise them." My visits to Ted's fruit and veg shop cheered me up no end. I love lovely bonkers people. I will not lie it was hard with Dominic's dad as he was very aggressive after a drink. The next day when he awoke he had little or no recall of it. But when I finally split up with him he gave up because I would not allow him to pick Dom up if he had a drink. He gave up for his son.

Eddie at my new job was a physic and had been on the television in one of the first reality Ghostbusters programme. His profile on Google reads (Albert Edward "Eddie" Burks [16 December 1922 – 23 August 2005]) was a civil engineer and self-proclaimed psychic who featured in the fourth episode of the first series of the television documentary *Ghost Hunters* in the episode entitled 'The Man Who Talks to Ghosts'. Burks' alleged extraordinary psychic powers made news headlines in 1993 when it was revealed that the Queen's bank Coutts contacted him to deal with a ghost at its prestigious Strand headquarters in Central London. His intervention is said to have laid to rest the troubled soul of Thomas Howard, 4th Duke of Norfolk who was executed for treason in 1572. Soon afterwards Eddie teamed up with freelance writer Gillian Cribbs to visit haunted places throughout England and act as a psychic therapist to troubled spirits. Eddie claimed to have contacted spirits in places as diverse as palaces, manor houses, pubs and council flats, while Gillian conducted interviews with witnesses and checked historical details. Gillian later went on to write the book *Ghost Hunter: Investigating the World of Ghosts and Spirits* in collaboration with Burks.)

He was the most down to earth person ever, no fancy stuff. It was really funny because it was the time of the children's film, *Ghostbusters,* which was a big hit and my son loved it. So when

Dominic heard me telling my friend I worked for Eddie Burks who was on the Ghost Hunters programme (basically he is a ghostbuster), he proudly boasted my mum works for a ghostbuster to all of his friends.

The job was lovely and as I had a troubled past, my perk of the job, was healing and counselling. Eddie used to place his hands on me and give me spiritual healing and I felt a lot better. We had all sorts of people come to stay, some very traumatized and other psychics.

I made some wonderful dishes even though I say so myself, perhaps I was channelling a chef who had left us but cooking did come naturally to me. For my bonus I got healing every day. Eddie had tuned in that I had been scalded when I was three and that I had trauma with my losing two fathers. So before work every morning he would heal me.

There was one man who did automatic writing and it was amazing he would sit at the table chatting whilst I was cooking and then he would go into a trance and just write on the piece of paper in front of him. When reading back he explained he was channelled by a girl from the Middle East who had been raped and died a horrible death and she needed to write it out. Eventually Eddie helped her go over to the other side. Eddie explained this girl was one of those people who got stuck between life and death because she did not want to meet her torturers so she would not go over. Also he explained some people are worried about moving on because of those they have left behind. I begged Eddie to take me on a Ghost Bust, but he refused. He said that I was too open as a person and I would need a lot of training to open and close. This is so you do not take on bad spirits he explained. He got a call one day from a local woman who thought she had a harmful ghost. When he came back, I excitedly ask him what happened. "Oh, Annette, you could have come to that one, as it was a cat which had died a long time ago. She had got shut in a cupboard. It was a very big cat who could not go over. He said, "The cat was so relieved when she went."

I worked there for as long as it existed and then Eddie was called to do other things. I understand Eddie died in 2000, I must say I was glad to have spent time with him and all his stories. You can find him explaining his releases as he called them on YouTube if you google Eddie Burkes' releases. You can hear his soft cockney voice. That was a very interesting job, suffice to say Eddie did eventually teach me to take people over and tune in.

ESTATE AGENCY PROPERTY DEVELOPING.

I had a lot of very good friends in Haslemere and some of them worried about my struggle. I started a part-time job at a local estate agency called Dixon and Dixon although there was only one Dixon, Martin Dixon who owned it. It seemed the workings were very similar to my employment agency work in London: a lot of record keeping and touting for business using the local press. I did quite well. I could always see the business and when bosses were not operating it properly. We had a lot of developers in Haslemere and one of them was renting the office below Martin. His name was Philip Rhodes and we sold his properties.

They were all hopeless time keepers and I had arranged a viewing on one of Philip's flats on the High Pavement in Haslemere. Philip had gone to play polo in Midhurst and taken the keys and I asked Martin if he had spare keys.

"No," he said, "You will just have to go and explain to the client."

"What am I going to say?" I asked.

"I don't know make something up," he said causally.

Off I went irritably. I arrived at the flat and a very well-to-do lady was waiting. On the way to the flat I had passed a ladder. I explained to the lady I had no keys but then saw a window open.

Then I said, "Do not worry I just passed a ladder. I will get it and climb in and open the door for you."

When I returned with the ladder to my surprise she insisted on climbing in herself. There seemed to be nothing I could do to stop her even though I argued. Up she went, then I heard a commotion, a dog barking, a man shouting and a thud, then I heard running down stairs, a door opened she appeared dishevelled and very angry and shouted at me.

"That's the wrong bloody flat I nearly got eaten by a dog."

She was followed by the owner who also shouted, "What are you playing at telling people to climb ladders and fall into my flat."

I stood there numb struck, sorry would have sounded so feeble. I checked she was all right, then a man came along and started shouting at me.

"Who has stolen my ladder? I went to get my car and came back – it had disappeared." I tried to explain but no one was listening.

They all threatened me with my boss, which I knew was pointless as he did not seem to care about anything.

Then I calmly said to the woman, "Would you like another appointment?"

To my surprise she said, "Yes."

I promised her I would call her when I had the keys in my hand. She bought the flat.

My career in Estate Agency continued, I went to work for an independent in Liphook. I enjoyed taking people around houses and selling a dream. I can visualise changes and how a house could look and that's what sells a house. It wasn't long before we were bought out by the Halifax so I ended up working for them. I had the most horrendous air hostess style green uniform to wear. It was the time of the eighties financial crash which was very interesting.

The credit card was a relatively new edition to our lives and all of a sudden we got letters coming through our doors saying we all could have credit cards, to me I saw danger. I had managed my finances so cleverly as I said, my best friend Tammy puts it you brought the children up on fresh air. I had no money but no debt. I could see that money cost money, but unfortunately a lot of people did not.

One particular family who lived opposite would go on mammoth shopping sprees with their new shiny credit card and come back with pointless things. It was like they had won the lottery, but they had to pay this money back. In those days the Chic was VW Golfs and yuppies with Filofaxs. They were big diaries with all you dates and appointments in, the fuller your Filofax the more successful you were perceived. If you were a true yuppie you always carried one around. It is really funny when you look back and yuppies always said, 'OK ya', even if they weren't public school educated.

I felt the economy was running on thin ice, people were spending what they had not got and would not be able to pay it back. It did not take a genius to work that out. Only a dyslexic.

So I stressed this to my friend who said, "Do not be silly it's booming it won't change. He had a Filofax and a VW and was a yuppy riding the crest of the yuppie wave. I told him about the neighbours across the road. I explained there is no money as they were already mortgaged up to the hilt so no money underneath them. It will not last, they would never be able to pay back their debts on credit cards. Who is going to pay?

He argued they could get another credit card, suffice to say they lost their house and had to move to a council house. I was so right it crashed. It was not just the neighbours across the road I saw people were borrowing up to the hilt buying the flashiest cars and bigger houses especially the middle classes. The credit had given them carte blanche to emulate the upper classes. OK ya.

Then it happened black Monday. Haslemere was commuter belt and it was hit badly. The debt was not under pinned. Marriages failed because deals had been made at the altar, where there is no love. The trade-off which had been made between bride and groom was over as the money was gone. Jobs were lost, mostly middle management. 'So the you give me a good life and I will be a good wife', although I might have an affair or two with a Mellor's type agreement, had failed. It was like the Palace of Versailles. Wives left the sinking ships like rats to find captains of ships that had not sunk. OK ya seemed to disappear.

I often referred to it as the all fur coat and no knickers syndrome. The no knickers being the lack of credit of course. How I sensed this in a society that was booming? But I knew it was going to happen. I do not know why but it was my housekeeping brain and I was right. I did not feel smug. I felt sad as they were dark times. There were a lot of depressed men hanging around bars saying their wives had left them as soon as they had lost their jobs, you see they had broken the deal. I think some of them secretly thought their wives actually loved them.

Well this crash was interesting, of course the housing crash hit the developers but they always tend to bounce back. If they were experienced they knew they had very profitable times ahead. They had to lose, but still had collateral.

Well I had already bought a flat next door to me on a buy to let. It had helped my financial situation no end. How did I do it? Well it was one of the first buy to let deals. I profited from the recession as the rental market increased. My mother had given Jim my brother some money and always gave us the same. So I used it for a deposit and rented the house next door to a tenant.

I was then working at the Halifax and it was hard going to sell in a recession. I asked if I could oversee a couple out of their repossessed house in Bordon. They were ex-military and had managed to buy their house. But the chap had lost his civilian job. The Halifax had given them a very short time to leave, as soon as the judge had banged his hammer done on an acquittal notice that was it. They were in a frantic panic when I arrived. I realised that I was the official on this occasion. (What would my careers advisor say now?) But rather than just standing there I helped them pack and gave them words of support. They were amazed. I negotiated them an extra few hours to decant all of their furniture. It was bad enough losing your house but not being able to get your possessions out in time would have been worse. I felt very sad for them they were going to family and friends.

I carried on working at the Halifax. I had a new boyfriend and I met some lovely new people. I was chatting to one of them one evening and said I wished I could buy and sell another house. "Have you ever bought one?" he asked.

"Yes I bought a buy to let and I am renting it."

"Well you can if you are confident. I loan pension funds. If you put together a good business plan I will loan, but and it is a big but, you have to turn the property quickly as the interest will be nine percent." I did my business plan, put in an offer and it all went through. At the time I was working at the Halifax part time and picking up three extra children after work and managing a property development. I took the kids after school. They played in the garden and I hit plaster off the walls, filled the skip and did the best I could. I then got the kids to bed and got babysitters and carried on. I tried to save money by doing the labouring as much as I could. I kicked the old ceiling plaster from upstairs from between the joists, then cleared the room, then had to get all of the nails from the beams. It was then and only then I discovered I could work really hard.

Then all of a sudden the estate agents hit the press because some of the estate agency world people were doing back to backs and it was all over the press. I did not know what a back to back was. I soon learnt it is where an estate agent buys a house and sells it before its completion date and completes simultaneously with purchase and vendor, therefore never having to pay for the house apart from the deposit. I actually had completed on my purchase in full with my pension fund backer and I was working like a dog so I could put it back on the market and sell within three months. Halifax head office heard that I had bought a house and sent down two Halifax in-house detectives. They took me into a room and proceeded to interrogate me very aggressively like good cop bad cop as though I was a criminal. They accused me of doing a back to back. I explained I had completed on it. They could see all the paperwork. It was quite an awful experience; they eventually ended the interview and then announced they would let me know if I could keep my job.

Suffice to say I lost it. I didn't mind I knew I had not done anything wrong as it said in the small print of our contracts that you could buy houses and sell them if you were employed by them, but you could not sell back to back they told me. They were worried the press would get hold of the story.

I sold the house successfully within three months and made some money to finally put in a decent kitchen and central heating into our own home. I must say I was really much healthier without central heating – never got colds.

I then had a little cash, and I had found a very good mechanic who used to teach me welding. I got chatting to him and he mentioned he wanted to buy and sell cars at the auction in Borden but he did not have the money. So we struck a deal. I would put up the money, he would do the work and we would split the profit. Our first car was a camper van which sold quickly, then an Audi, and then a BMW 1000 a beautiful car. I drove round in it until we sold it but unfortunately it had an alloy head gasket. If we had checked all the rubber tubes in the car we would have been fine but they were gone and the car overheated and broke down. So he had to skim the head, change all the rubbers and it was fine – we made a good profit,

I had chosen another boyfriend who was dysfunctional and we split up. My daughter was about to go to university and my son was going to secondary and I felt like a big move.

STAINED GLASS COURSE AND COMMISSIONS

I was always doing something creative in my spare time. I never felt at ease unless I was making or planning something, that is why I often burnt the lentils. I had always loved glass so Eleanor and I decided to do a stained glass course in West Dene College near Midhurst. It was a three-day course. The course was run by Paul San Cascani, who had been doing stained glass for many years. It was wonderful. First the house and the grounds were extraordinary, the mansion West Dene in the rolling countryside of Sussex. I loved the glass. We were given a simple template to work with. Firstly we had to learn to cut glass with scrap glass. Then we were let loose on the real pieces. Then after cutting we had to lead the panel up. The lead has to be stretched and then cut to fit the pieces. Then soldering so it all gels together. I loved it I was so proud of my first panel. That was it I was hooked. I bought the tools you needed to set up at home: a soldering iron, a wizard machine which helps you shape the glass when cut slightly wrong, grozers and the most important glass cutter. Then I started making panels. My first panel was given to me as a challenge – make anything you want for my window for a price. It was a big panel and it was very well received. Then Eleanor and I made a beautiful panel for a lady in George Street in Godalming. I mention this commission as I think we achieved almost the impossible. She wanted a long panel with delicate wild flowers. Stained glass is far from delicate so we used the Tiffany copper foiling method to create the delicate section. It looked so beautiful. I made quite a bit in that time for different people, also doing leaded light repairs. My children also both had a go and were very good at cutting and leading as I had my studio in the middle room of our three-storey house.

So as I said Angelique had a place at university. I was so proud. Dominic was going up to secondary school so I could consider moving and having a new chapter of my life.

Chapter Nine

Moving to Bath and Starting a Business

Looking back, my most important job in the world ever will always be bringing up my two children. So I did not regret the jobs I did around them so that I could be home for them after school. In fact it was a real honour. This gave me the opportunity to spend time with them. Having no qualifications leaves you a bit light on real career opportunities to earn a good salary. This is why I was hell-bent on my children going to university. I wanted them to have good opportunities and choices in life. My daughter did go but my son did not want to, that was his choice and it was a good choice as universities had become a more expensive option with student loans instead of grants. He would have needed to borrow, he argued.

"Why should I create debt when I don't know what I want to be yet? But I know I don't want unnecessary debt."

I knew he would be successful in whatever he did because he is really clever, works hard and has a bounty of common sense. He is now earning a very big salary and is married to beautiful Natalie who is now a junior doctor.

My mother always said the best thing you can give your children is independence. I now think she is spot on, 'groom them for life'.

She did that with us as she was worried how we would cope if she died as we had no one else. We are all far from perfect and we are all here to learn lessons. I tried to teach my children that mistakes were a path to wisdom. Mistakes teach you, if you keep making the same mistakes it is your choice not to learn from them. I had to make several mistakes over and over until I learnt.

The stained glass course I did had been successful and I started to develop a little business in Haslemere, working on small commissions for local people.

My daughter had successfully applied for a place at a university in Yorkshire and I suddenly found my life was at a crossroads. She is now a music coordinator and teacher and has her own music academy. Her marriage is successful to Steve who is now a master glassmaker and a wonderful husband to her.

She said to me the other day, "Mum you know I really enjoyed it when we were poor we had so much fun." I was so touched.

She wrote me this poem on Mother's Day last year.

Mum

When she laughs her face shines

Her hair is soft and blonde like an angel

My beautiful mum lights up the room

Her eyes twinkle with a tapestry of stories

I am so proud of her – she achieves great things

She is brimming with ideas and brave enough to do them

Thank you for inspiring creating and loving me

Angelique Williamson

Now if you said to me you can swap your life to a life of academia and be a great scholar, I would say no because that poem to me is better than any qualification or certificate of achievement. My daughter and son are both very successful and happy loving people. That is the best form of academic degree I could have, a BA in Life with honours!

One of the memories we laugh about are the games we played when we were skint. Our favourite one is the one we played with Tammy, my best friend, who also lived in Haslemere. We called it 'Not now Kato'.

It was a game to help cheer the children on boring shopping trips. We all loved the film *The Pink Panther*. In the film Inspector Clouseau played by Peter Sellers, has a Chinese Kung Fu expert as his butler, who is teaching him the art of Kung Fu. He tells him to attack him anytime so that he can practise his moves to defend himself. So Kato is always leaping out on him but at the wrong times, for example he leaps out of the wardrobe when he is making love to a beautiful woman.

He shouts,

"NOT NOW KATO!"

Our supermarket game involved one of us going on ahead in the aisles and then jumping out to surprise the others. You would have to leap out, make Kung Fu gestures and shout, "Attack!"

Dom was only little, just three or so but loved being in the trolley watching the crazy antics of his Aunty Tammy, his mum and sister.

Leekie was very good at surprising us.

One day in Somerfields whilst on one such boring shopping trip, Tammy went on ahead past the cereals as Kato. We turned into the bread aisle and looked down to the end to see if she was hiding. We looked behind and all around but there was no sign of her.

We looked up to the end of the aisle where there was a Japanese woman with her friend walking towards the next section. Then as if in slow motion we watched as Tammy leapt out right in front of them making Kung Fu gestures shouting, "ATTACK!"

OMG I could not breathe for laughing so much.

Tammy was dying with embarrassment as little Dominic shouted out, "NOT NOW KATO!"

Tears rolled down our faces as the poor shocked Japanese lady proceeded into the wine and beer section closely holding on to her companion.

We walked towards her to explain Tammy's actions and stifling our giggles we tried to tell her it was a game that we played. It was lost in translation, suffice to say she was not amused.

Other games we played included guess the advert whilst watching television, the winner being the first one who could correctly identify and shout out what the advert was advertising before it was shown. Great fun for us as we didn't have the sonic, the hedgehog games or other 'in' games that others could afford.

Dominic was a beautiful child with blond locks but he had ADHD which I always pronounce as ADHT. It was because he had a very active mind, loads of energy and batteries which never switched off. But he was an angel at school thank goodness. Now he has the calmest composure of anyone I have ever met.

My boyfriend at that time was a developer and had recently completed a deal on the property Heytesbury House near Warminster which I would visit with Dominic at weekends.

My friend Nick came down and stayed at Heytesbury for the weekend and we took a trip to Bath. The last time I was in Bath was the 1960s. We used to go swimming in the Roman Baths with my mum and dad before they were closed.

They closed them to the public because of a link to meningitis in the 1970s. Apparently, according to my mother, the first visit I just ran from the changing room and jumped into to the waters and my dad had to rescue me. I remember the Baths even though I was so young. It was great to see Bath again. We walked around Bath, had coffee in Waterstones in Milson Street and I fell back in love with the city.

Most people who come to Bath love it. Even on days when the weather is grim you can wander the streets, take strength from the water at the weir, marvel at the architecture and on a really cold day walk along the cobblestones by the Cross Baths and see the steam rising mysteriously out through the cobblestones in the road. It is really quite magical. This is one of my favourite places as it is the source of the hot springs.

Being from nearby Bristol I setteled soon as I moved back there, I had not felt like this in years. So being back in the West Country felt like home to me after living in the south east for so long. It felt much better. My great, great grandfather got married in Bath Abbey and on his death certificate it says that he died in James Street, West Bath.

I was at a crossroads with my relationship, it was going nowhere with the developer (another book). I was chatting to my brother telling him I loved Bath. He had returned to Bristol and he had re-started Bristol Blue Glass, and suggested we opened a shop in Bath together.

With great excitement I said, "Yes."

Although it was a big move with Angelique at University and Dominic moving to secondary school it seemed like the timing was perfect. So Jimmy and I set about finding a shop. The first one we looked at was in Kingsmead Square which did not feel right.

We finally looked at one in Broad Street, parallel with Milsom Street, a main thoroughfare and full of High Street shops. It was a bit off the beaten track but was available for a manageable rent. Bath then was still recovering from the recession and the hotel The Royal York at the top of Broad Street was derelict and the shops were a bit shabby.

On my first visit I sat opposite waiting for the lady from Bath council in the chocolate shop on the opposite side of the road. The owner had a grey depressed look about him and the girl serving looked like Morticia from the Addams family. I asked her what the passing trade was like. She was honest and told me it was not brilliant but it's OK.

I sat drinking my coffee staring at the shop I wanted and fantasising about being in there. It was a handmade paper shop called Papyrus, which had been successful and was now moving to a shop nearer to the city centre.

The lady from the council arrived, introduced me to the owners and she showed me around. It was amazing; it was over five floors. As you entered the shop it had a front section with an antique fire grate and then the stairs divided it into two halves. Upstairs was a makeshift kitchen for the staff and a store room which was also divided by the stairs. Up again were more storage rooms and up again a bathroom and another room with a beautiful Victorian fireplace. The owners informed me they had enjoyed living there for five years but moved offsite a while back. She then showed me out onto a mini roof terrace where you could see all over Bath. They told me they had barbecues there. I was to have some lovely moments up there too. My brother arrived and we put in an offer for the shop which was accepted.

I let my house out in Haslemere to a religious group. The date for completion on the shop was delayed so I had to go and live with my mother in Eltham SE London for two weeks. The date came for me to move into the shop. I drove down to Bath in a 2CV with two dogs and my son and a car full of duvets. This was a massive step for me as I had friends in Haslemere and knew nobody in Bath at all.

My mum waved me off with tears in her eyes, worried for my future.

We arrived at 25 Broad Street. It was quite dark and Jim arrived at the same time .We opened the shop door and walked in.

I could have cried, there was paper everywhere. It was an absolute mess, filthy in fact. I had my furniture arriving shortly and had to make space to put it. Jim had to go to his partner as he was having problems.

So Dominic and I set to clear one room for beds and one for storage. I look back and I am so proud of him. He was eleven and worked so hard alongside me. My mum came down at the weekend and cried again at the state of the place and bought me a cooking ring as we had no cooker. But I am always up for a challenge and Dominic and I worked hard to get it right. Also Dominic was loving the takeaways. Jim helped with the shop and sent his friend Sarah up from Exmoor to help me, as I had no retail experience whatsoever, so she taught me window display. When they had all gone I realised I did not even know where a hardware shop was. I had to learn everything the hard way. Google did not exist, that is why I love the internet you can go anywhere now and find the shops you need, in fact whatever you need. It makes all of us a lot more independent. I felt really alone scared and wondered whether I had done the right thing. I was missing my friends, most of all one of my best friends, Phil.

The first day opening the shop I was excited and all alone. I sat there and waited for customers. I think a few people walked in but not many. I was so disappointed. Having never been in retail I was completely naïve. Then it dawned on me nobody knew I was there. I had to do marketing. So I deliberated in my head, the nearest footfall was in Milsom Street, the Street parallel with Broad Street.

I needed to do a leaflet and distribute it so I asked my brother to make me a glass hat. He got his mate Pete Sinclair to make it and Pete's daughter Anna was looking for a job part time so I took her on and went out leafleting. It brought people in. I also flyered Broad Street car park which worked until I was banned by the council as it was their car park.

But on the second night of my opening I was lying in bed. Dom was in his bed asleep and there was an almighty crash. I ran downstairs and someone had smashed our shop window. I called the police. Dom came down too. It was very frightening. But I have a motto I always had to use: 'out of crisis comes opportunities'. So I called the local paper and told them indignantly, "Is this how people welcome people to Bath with a new venture?" I got very good press. With the press article in the local paper and the leaflets the shop became known and busy. Stained-glass commissions started to come in. Glass started selling.

Unfortunately my brother's relationship was breaking down. I was a year into the business and things were going well, and I needed someone to run the stained-glass department, as it was all a bit much. Jim said he had bumped into a guy who had given him his CV. He had just finished at Swansea University doing a stained-glass degree. He gave me his number. Two days later I picked up the phone and a strange thing happened: Themis the applicant also was walking towards the phone to call me. So as I phoned he was picking up the phone to call me.

Themis came for an interview and took the job as workshop manager. Guess what? He too is dyslexic!

Needless to say we hit it off immediately. He was and is an excellent salesperson. His training was hard-core; he had done door-to-door sales to earn money to fund his stained-glass degree. He was good with customers and we understood each other as we both had dyslexic experiences. I was settling in gradually, getting to meet people in Bath.

Shortly after I arrived and before the shop opened, I was painting inside in my dungarees and happened to look out of the window and noticed a man peering in. He had Marc Bolan curly locks and was having a good look through the window. I thought he looked nice and smiled at him as he suddenly noticed I had seen him.

A few weeks later when I was open, he came into the shop and introduced himself as a fellow shopkeeper, who had a shop in Walcot Street called Adrenalin High which sold specialist outdoor gear and equipment. He told me he was a member of 'The Real Shops' campaign.

"We are a collective of independent businesses who are trying to preserve the independent shops in Bath. There is a fee but you are then entered into a booklet which is distributed to hotels and the tourist information office," he told me.

I jumped at it and signed up.

In a short time the curly haired man from 'The Real Shops' Campaign had become a close friend.

On the first Christmas Eve he invited me out for a drink, so I got a sitter and went around to his shop. He was just cashing up and there in front of the till was a girl.

Seeing me come through the shop door he said, "I'll be around at the Pig and Fiddle in a minute. Michael, my friend, is there go and talk to him."

I did and met Michael who it turns out had grown up near Haslemere, so we chatted.

Adrian, the curly-haired man, did not turn up for ages.

I now know that he had been in deep conversation with the young girl and finishing with her, which I didn't realise at the time. So when he turned up and I went to talk to him to tell him I had to go she stood in front of me and glared. So I gave up on him even being a friend as I assumed he was taken.

Adrian pursued me after that and we became good friends. There after developed what I call 'The Real Bath Shop' love affair.

Adrian was often popping in my shop to see me. We were only friends for ages. He helped with Dominic and got on well with him. He was a runner and an athlete. He eventually used to babysit for me as I had decided to go out to a singles night at the Red Car Hotel just off Great Pultney Street. I wanted to meet people, it was not for dating as I had had enough of relationships and felt I was no good at them. He has since told me that he was anxious all that night that I would meet someone. Of course I didn't, as everyone was so much older than me.

Our relationship developed as friends and one day I was invited out to a Valentines do with a friend of a friend from Haslemere. I was unclear if it was a date or not, so I asked, "Do I come alone or bring someone?"

"That's up to you."

"What does that mean?" I replied.

He mumbled and stumbled and gave me a load of waffle, so I thought in that case I would take my friend Adrian to be safe.

I often gave my dogs a stretch in the square around the back of my shop which was just between Broad Street and Walcot Street. This particular night I was waiting for Adrian the night before the Valentines do. He appeared from around the corner. The sun was on him, he looked tanned from his running.

"Hi!" I said.

Saying nothing he walked straight up to me and kissed me.

Wow! My heart pounded, that was it then.That night we went to the Bell in Walcot Street, and chatted, he talked with animation about his beautiful daughter Alice. We shared children stories, and he obviously loved her as much as I loved mine. We had a few glasses.

Two things I was good at from school was art and walking on my hands. As we walked back towards my shop we were laughing, he asked if there was anything he needed to know about me.

"Yes!" I said, "I am useless at relationships, I am dyslexic and I can walk on my hands."

He laughed.

I protested. "I'll show you!" and then proceeded to walk along Walcot Street beside him on my hands.

Adrian, being competitive in most things, then launched onto his hands trying to copy me. Of course he could not compete and I stood there laughing at him as he kept trying. I kept walking on my hands as he was wobbling all over the place falling over and trying again.

Then I looked up and the people from the flats opposite were staring at us. Two adults doing handstands at eleven thirty at night under the streetlights. We giggled and ran up the steps by the YMCA to my flat above the shop.

Now Adrian and I came together with what people call baggage. I have this vision in my head as dyslexics think in pictures. It is a cartoon with us facing each other both with our hands holding a rope over our shoulders pulling a massive pile of trunks behind us, with a balloon over each of us saying, "I'm fine, I haven't got baggage."

Of course coming together in later life our trunks we were pulling were chocka block with previous relationships and childhood anxieties… OMG is all I can say.

It is completely another story but suffice to say we are still together today after twenty years and, because we found love, we both decided we did not want to lose it and we took ourselves to relationship counselling, and finally I consider myself quite good at relationships but now but I cannot walk on my hands any more.

From the little shop in Broad Street we developed Bath Aqua Glass. We chose the colour after a lot of research. The glass is coloured with copper oxide which is reminiscent of the Bath Spa waters. It is a beautiful Aqua colour which is synonymous with Bath. We also adorned it with trails as the Romans did which represented eternal health. It is often called snake thread ware or serpent ware. The snake is the symbol of the Hippocratic oath of medicine.

Bath Aqua Glass grew. The day we launched with the Mayor of Bath in our little shop in Broad Street. We dressed in togas and so many people came, some had to stay outside the shop. We were featured on BBC local news programme *Points West.*

The shop became more and more well known and eventually we went over the VAT threshold and I had to do a VAT return. I had as advised saved all of my receipts to do with the business. I filled in the VAT form as best I could, and lived in fear as other people in business had said the VAT office are worse than the police. If you get it wrong you can be jailed. Being not at one with authoritive judgment I was terrified.

The VAT office, I can say through bitter experience, is not the bogey man it is often portrayed to be.

Now the way I had stored my receipts was spiked with a big needle and a large roll of string with a knot at the end and I had put them on in date order. That seemed logical to me. It looked like a large paper snake. After I had submitted my return as best I could, the VAT office phone me up and asked me about my VAT return. I explained it was my first time and I had done my best, he told me the figures were totally nonsensical and there was something very wrong. I was terrified, he told me not to worry and he would come out and help. The guy up the road in the hairdressers put the fear of God in me. He told me if they come to visit you, you're in trouble, so all that week I was in a state of anxiety, not sleeping.

The VAT man arrived and he was lovely. He asked me to get my receipts and my daily takings day sheets. He was sitting at the table in the kitchen and I returned with my paper snake and day sheets.

He could not stop laughing.

"You creative types!" he said.

Then he sat with me and showed me how to list them in different categories month by month. We successfully filled in the VAT return. As it turned out they actually owed me a little, as with a new business you have set up costs. I felt a great deal of relief, he told me he could not do this every time but if the business keeps on going like this I should get an accountant and a bookkeeper. I had a good night's sleep that night.

My brother split up with his long-term partner and needed to buy her out and Themis my stained glass manager wanted to buy into a business. I thought long and hard, he was such a good salesman I thought it would be a good idea. So he bought Jim's share.

We constantly needed marketing ideas to keep us in the press as we were off the main high street and I came up with some corkers.

Bath has a fringe festival and I went to a fringe meeting and there was already in existence an alternative fashion show which was raising money for save the whales and dolphins. I had a meeting with Nick who was running it and told him I would like to design glass dresses and outfits for the show. It was a great success. We all worked hard to make clothes out of glass for the show. I did some press releases and we were on main BBC breakfast television walking through central Bath being filmed in the Roman Baths in the most original and stunning clothing. It was a great success. Both my son and daughter were models as was I, Themis and most of the staff. It was such a fun evening. Adrian who is a natural showman was our compere.

The following year we were involved in the Alternative Fashion Show again. This year it was in a bar at the top of town and the manager got it sponsored by Red Bull. So I designed a polo costume out of empty Red Bull cans and it was featured in the press. All of this marketing worked and it was great fun.

We had a work experience boy, James, who was really shy and who showed a talent for stained glass. We took him on as a Saturday boy. His mum was so pleased as he too was dyslexic and she was really worried about him. He was persuaded to be a model for the fashion show. Themis encouraged him by giving him some Red Bull shots but just before he was supposed to go out on the catwalk, as his music came on, he walked towards the door and threw up. So I had to throw on another dress and go out. Which confused our compere Adrian as I appeared in an outrageously low cut number to the tune of 'You Shook Me All Night Long' by AC/DC whilst expecting the young James to be prancing about in his macho glass outfit! It wasn't just eyes popping out that night!

The business grew as new businesses appeared in Bath including a new radio company called Bath FM which a lot of local people started to listened to.

I was driving in my car one particular day and this most awful advert came on with this chap talking in a very broad West Country accent.

"I'm Alan Joy the winder man. Remember Alan Joy the winder man!" which was accompanied by some dodgy music.

I cringed and laughed at the same time, but out of all the adverts I noticed I remembered it and talked to my friends about it. This gave me an idea.

I rushed back to the shop excited and announced to Themis that we were going to do our own radio advert. So we found a guy with some equipment to record the advert and it was done.

It was awful.

I know this because people came in to the shop and complained about it.

So it worked… it was noticed!

We did a sketch in which I was a lady who needed a stained glass panel and Themis came around to measure up the stained-glass window and sell it to me. Delighting about the benefits of a stained-glass window and as he was leaving I said in the most annoying suggestive voice, "Would you like a coffee?" We were taking the mickey out of that coffee advert at that time which was causing quite a stir.

It was very funny, every time we heard it we cried laughing. We got a lot of stained-glass commissions from that ad.

One customer came in cursing the advert and shouted, "Ask them to take it off!!"

I tried to explain it was contracted in for a certain amount of time and we had paid for it.

"Whose voice is it?" he asked.

I told him it was mine. I suggested that he could always turn it off or listen to another radio station.

As he calmed he began to look around the shop and bought something.

So the marketing lesson I had learnt from Alan Joy Windows was to be annoying and get noticed.

Another idea came to me when The Bath International Music Festival was holding a Best Dressed Window Competition for the shops in Bath. Among the categories was the 'Most over the top window'. It was the festival's innovative way to promote itself because if you entered you had to display a Bath Festival poster. So we came up with the idea of the glass bikini.

We got one made and persuaded our lovely Swedish friend Lydia who had an amazing figure, to stand in the window on Bath Festival launch day with both Themis and I in togas.

We all had lutes and Lydia, a trainee teacher, had just been on a placement in Africa and taught us some African songs to play and sing.

By this time my mother had moved to Corsham near Bath and was helping in the shop part time. She did not always agree with my wacky ideas in fact she would often say, "You can't do that, Annette!"

That was always like a red flag to a bull to me, nobody told me what I could or couldn't do after those people at school who got me so wrong.

"You can't work in an office la la la…"

Don't get me wrong, I loved my mum but we were different.

So on the day, we emptied the window of stock, put a sheet up as backdrop and Themis, Lydia and myself took to the window.

We had people outside all day with an array of bemused, amused and confused faces.

The judges were due to arrive at the shop at three and the anticipation was rising but my mum, who was manning the shop, was becoming more and more hysterical.

"GET OUT OF THAT WINDOW!" she shouted. "You are destroying this business! How can we take money when you are cavorting half naked making that racket in the window?"

"Mum," I called out from the window over the drones of Themis singing and Lydia plucking a lute, "It's marketing!"

"Why can't you do anything normal?" she replied.

"What's wrong with just putting adverts in the paper? And please stop singing… you're tone deaf! It sounds terrible!"

Well the evidence was there to say she was wrong. Much to her annoyance, customers came in and bought more than on a usual day.

She berated me all day in front of them and they laughed.

It was a bit like a scene in the Monty Python film 'Life of Brian'… "Annette, get out of that window, you naughty girl!"

I did not mind as I loved her dearly. When the judges turned up their faces were a picture, as they gazed in amazement at the scene in the window.

We won 'most over the top' window.

Marketing has changed now, it was so much fun in those days. As the business grew so did the challenges, employing people was a learning curve to me. When you are new to employment you want to be everybody's friend and you soon learn this is not the case. Also I thought everyone knew more than me which was stupid. It is just like life, you gel with some people and others you find you do not gel with. I will give you two scenarios of my first experiences.

I interviewed a girl for a sales position who was really upbeat: she had had experience of selling and seemed perfect for the job. The first two weeks she was OK, then it began. She started crying for no reason. I tried to console her but to no avail.

Then she announced that she had fibromyalgia which I found out was a form of ME. She started becoming very down and this hampered her selling. Eventually she phoned in sick one day and asked me to pick up some medication from her doctor but I would have to call him first. The doctor was very distressed and said I needed to go to her flat with the medication and check her weight as she was anorexic and often got down to a dangerous weight. I delivered her medication and she looked very gaunt, so I called the doctor who had her hospitalised and put on a drip. I learnt that my interviewing techniques needed to improve, although I found this very difficult as generally we all put on a good show for an interview.

The second experience was again for a sales assistant/bookkeeper, again it was a female who seemed extremely efficient as it all started well. Her efficiency was well received and I felt pleased to share some of the load as the business was growing. But after about three weeks she became dictatorial. Started treating me like her employee, so much so I dreaded going to work.

Being dyslexic, people can find you chaotic but as my mother always said 'people underestimate you, that is always their mistake.'

It became unbearable and then I started to notice that my cash was not balancing as I was in charge of the petty cash. I got everyone who worked for me in a room and gave a speech. "You may think I am chaotic," I began, "but I know my business inside out. I started it and I know that money is going missing."

I continued, "I am not accusing anybody but I am just letting you know I am watching. The books need to balance and we need to make money each week to pay the wages so if anyone is stealing they are stealing from themselves and their colleagues."

Then this particular girl started shouting, "Are you accusing me?"

"No I'm not," I replied. "I'm just giving a general warning across the board."

I explained, "I can't accuse anybody but monies are missing!"

"You're accusing me!" she shouted indignantly. "That's it I'm leaving"

Everyone looked very shocked. She grabbed her things and stormed out. I asked everyone if they had felt accused by my speech. None of them did. So all I could think was that she was not completely honest. I was relieved as I could look forward to going to work again.

The business grew and we had our first workshop on Walcot Street. It was a bit off the beaten track. It had holes in the roof and when we did a glass-blowing demonstration if it was raining it would come through onto the workshop area. At times this required the glassblowers to hold an umbrella over the piece of work being made, much to the amusement of visitors. After a couple of years the site was sold by our landlord and we needed to move. A year previous to this Adrian sold his share in Adrenalin High and bought into Bath Aqua Glass and joined me in the running of the bussiness.

A factory came up on the main street of Walcot Street. It was a lot more money. Adrian knew the landlord and we met up with him. He was lovely and has been a great landlord. He is Erling Jenson. He was a racing driver and was great friends with Jenson Button's dad and Jenson was named after him.

The building had previously been a garage. We also decided to get some professional furnace builders in: Jacob and Bjorn Svenson who had help build the Dartington Glass furnaces in Devon. They were a pair of delightful Swedes always keen to help and very keen for us to succeed.

I was relieved they were building them as our furnaces were a pain in the ass. If we changed the pot which held the glass for melting, one of us would have to sit with the furnace all night or most of the night at least and watch it gradually reach the correct temperature. We were all tired of taking it in turns, staying up all night waiting for the 1200 degrees centigrade melting temperature to be reached at so many degrees per minute. The furnace runs at 1100 degrees, at that time we melted rod end from Dartington. Which is the waste from their glass blowing.

Jacob lived in Torrington and had worked with Dartington for years as had Bjorn who had since returned to Sweden, having set up a Specialist Electronics company. They were sad about how Dartington had changed in recent years. As they said as soon as the suits (city investors) stepped in and bought it everything changed. The in-house creativity had gone. I understand what they meant and thought I wanted to keep Bath Aqua as a hand-made in Bath product and not out source it to China. Which was a hard thing to do, because at that time China was flourishing, factories were popping up everywhere, copying and manufacturing everything.

We were competing but we, both my brother with Bristol Blue and us at Bath Aqua stuck to our guns. We both went through some rocky rides.

The idea of Adrian joining the business seemed wonderful but any couple who have run a business will tell you it is madness.

The power struggle began. We are both headstrong, in fact people often underestimate Adrian, he has a heart of gold but if you cross him that is it, he will cut you out of his life. Whatever you try to do. He will fight for our children and he is one of the most loving people and the hardest workers I have met.

We fought and we fought some more, we hardly agreed on anything, often we were both arguing the same point in different ways. I was fiercely independent as I had been in charge of the ship carrying myself Dom and Leeks. So that caused difficulties.

Themis, Adrian and I became the three Musketeers, we fought we laughed but it was only the other day that I realised we did all of those things because we had a passion for our business, if you have no passion there is nothing. No business.

Adrian and I got to the stage where we were going to split up, things had become unbearable, but there was a deep love between us and a lot of passion. So we decided to go to counselling it was the best thing we ever did. We unpacked our baggage week by week, started to communicate without having to score points. One morning we were sitting in bed, my favourite time of the day with him. We have our little chats, no business is spoken. It is banned from the bedroom.

He looked at me and said, "We are finally alone in this bed! Isn't it wonderful, all of our exes have gone." I gave him the biggest cuddle ever. He used to joke there are eight people in this bed before counselling, but it was true we both had issues with exes. That was a wonderful day when we realised we were finally a relatively balanced secure couple with trust.

Our business grew.

We had moved to 105-107 Walcot Street, then another recession hit, in fact it felt like the plague of Egypt. We had borrowed a lot of money for the move and put our properties up as security. The UK was firstly hit by the mad cow disease, bovine spongiform, CJD. On our TV one night there was a film with thousands of carcasses being burnt, with talk of it spreading to humans. This went out worldwide. It looked like the UK was in darkness. The tourists stopped coming and our takings dropped. Some Americans came into the studio to watch the glass blowing demonstrations. They told us all their friends had cancelled their trips, they were not eating beef. We cut down the hours of our staff to manage. The next thing to hit that hit our local trade was foot and mouth; the country saw 2,000 cases of the disease in farms across most of the British countryside. Over ten million sheep and cattle were killed in an eventually successful attempt to halt the disease Cumbria was the worst affected area of the country, with 843 cases. All county shows and even Cheltenham races were cancelled. By the time that the disease was halted in October 2001, the crisis was estimated to have cost the United Kingdom £8bn (US$16bn). This was also aired by the media worldwide.

What next could hit us and the world? Well in 2001 on September 11 we all remember that fateful day. It was unbelievable. What can you say? But give a thought for everyone who perished that day and their families. Our business problems were insignificant compared to what they were going through. But we still had to soldier on. The Americans were not going to travel now. A friend of mine, Lyn Moorhouse, decided to make a very brave statement, she had been in an air-crash and survived and she was terrified of flying. She decided to fly to New York as a memorial to the people who lost their lives and to show the terrorists we would not be afraid. She had a meeting planned with

Mayor Rudy Giuliani. She asked us if we would blow a commemorative piece for her to take for the people of New York, which we did and she very bravely flew there. I took my hat off to Lynn because I know it was a massive statement.

All of these events stopped tourists coming to Bath, so my housekeeping skills had to step in running a business on fresh air. Sleepless nights when then banks would not lend when wages were due. But we stuck in there. We used the credit card that I hated, but we used them cleverly. It was actually a very efficient way of loaning money, if you always paid on time, and also balance transfers had started to come into fruition so we used them. My brother always said the banks give you umbrellas when it is sunny but when it is raining they take them away. It was difficult times but we beat the banks, they foreclosed on a lot of good businesses at that time.

I must say the tax office was good in the recession if you let them know what was going on. They waited for funds and worked with me to keep the business going. I did have to fight for it but when you explained the situation they conceded.

By now I had the work experience's boy James', mother, Judith, working with me. She had run a stall for us in Castle Market, Trowbridge for a few years. We finally closed it and she came to work in Bath. Judith is now my factory manager and she runs it very efficiently. She has been through many a crisis with us. She has even waited for wages to cash flow us through. Her son James was funded by Councillor Peter Metcalf and apprenticed with us as a glass blower. He now has his own studio having gone to university and worked at the Royal Academy. He is also a great dyslexic success story.

Working with me is not easy; my staff have called me the hurricane amongst other things. I work at a fast pace and people are always telling me I have so much energy. Judith and I have an honest relationship. She can tell me when she is not happy with certain things. For example my mind works very fast and if have an idea I want it to appear. So I would often turn up at the glass blowing studio with an idea, interrupt the blowers, discuss it with them and get them making it. Judith would be livid as she had set out the production schedule, which had deadlines, and I had totally mucked it up.

So I had to listen, that is necessary when you give responsibilities to people and want them to manage your production. So we devised a system, I discussed it with Jude at our weekly meetings and then it went into the schedule.

Now there is a thing called weekly meetings. I had to get used to them as I hated them. I now like them. Before Adrian came along in the business, Themis' motto and mine was 'to think is to do', both being dyslexic this worked. With a small amount of people it worked. But when Adrian came along he always remarked that I would go from A to Z and miss out the middle. He likes to think about things, dot the I's and cross the T's, and in his earlier life he was a teacher. One of his angry jibes was 'and it is because of the way you and Themis operate'. Eventually through our accountant we looked at our strengths and weaknesses and defined roles. We structured in weekly meetings, which in the beginning were a nightmare, as Ade and I had not started counselling. So we introduced the wooden talking spoon to the meetings, whoever had the spoon could talk and the others had to listen. Judith was so patient with us. The passion at the meetings prevailed but they got better and better.

Adrian announced one day that he was jealous of our dyslexia because of the creative process; it was so funny. We nominated him as a fellow dyslexic. But if you are not one naturally it is hard to be one especially if you do not agree with the TO THINK IS TO DO MOTTO. I love him the way he is.

I had really met my Mr Darcy.

Chapter Ten

The Wedding

My mother had become ill. Adrian and I took a long time to get married, as marriage to us had not been a positive experience. He had lost his father at the age of nine. His mother had not married again and brought her children up solo. Then me losing two fathers, one to divorce and one to death, after my mother had married him, gave me a morbid fear of it. I actually believed if I got married I would be deserted or become a widow. It took a bit of counselling to sort this.

So we finally decided to marry and we both wanted my mum there. If we could orchestrate a wedding in Corsica we could plan one in six weeks here. My mother loved talking about it.

We got the banns read and booked the registrar's office, but decided we wanted a hand fasting in our garden across the road, which we called the paddock. So we invited just close family and friends to the registry office and the rest to the hand fasting. I had invited my best friend from school, Janice, and her husband Dave, who now lived in Perth Australia. I did not for one minute think they would come. But they did. The date was set 12th February 2011. Our friend lent us a marquee and we bedecked it with the February foliage. My daughter arranged for her choir to sing a beautiful Native American tribe song 'Shooshan'. I had Tammy, Janice, Angelique and Matilda as bridesmaids. I wore a dress of

King Arthur period style. The whole thing was beautiful. Jimmy gave me away and we walked into the marquee to 'Shooshan' and there was my mum looking so beautiful, her eyes sparkling. Adrian was in an Irish kilt, along with my son and Steve also in kilts.

I had asked the universe for a good sunny day, it was the sunniest day I had ever seen in winter. Adrian had made a Corsican style arch for the marquee. When I entered and stood there I was in heaven. Adrian made his speech and cried… I made mine. We had come so far. Debbie, my daughter's sister-in-law, sang 'Fields of Gold' and Adrian and I led everyone hand in hand up to the golf course to the reception in a marquee. On the way up Adrian sang 'I Will Walk Five Hundred Miles' to me all the way. I loved it, it so was magical.

My cousin drove my mum up. She sat bedside me on the top table. I had arranged a surprise for her. Tom, the love of her life who she lost, was a Frank Sinatra fan and used to sing 'My Way'. She loved it. The best man had a great voice and sang 'My Way' to my mum and she loved it. She actually stayed until ten o'clock which was a surprise. We rocked until we dropped and Adrian's best friend Jerry played with his band. My mother talked about it for weeks.

My mother deteriorated, so Adrian and I moved in with her lock stock and barrel. As I had pledged she was not going into hospital. I wanted my mum to be treated like a queen. She had suffered enough through her childhood and life with events. Both Jimmy and I worked out a plan so we could care for her. He still had young Tilly and he was being let down at Bristol Blue by staff. Even at that time when his mum was dying, he did two days and nights a week stay over and I did the rest. We had the help of

Dorothy House, the hospice care in our area. They were magnificent. I am so glad I cared for her. Mum and I were so different but in that period she told me she was proud of me. I can tell you I was so proud of her. She took no painkillers. Her argument was 'I want all my faculties'. She had run her own life tight up to the time she died, as she had no-one, except Tom for a short period, to lean on and he was ripped from her.

I loved every minute of being with her at the end of her life because I think we treasured the moments. We were in the now knowing that was all we had. We talked for hours.

Mum was still in complete control, if we left a light on in a room we were not in she would scream to turn off the light. Or if we turned the heating up, she would turn it down. This came from her childhood, the war years, where everything was precious. It still is but we are less aware. She was right if everyone in the country did this we would save a fortune in energy use. It dawned on me that it is such a short time from the war yet we have become so wasteful in many parts of our lives. Mum would send me up to the shops with her visa card and give me instructions. I was careful not to confront her and take over as I had done that with my will too inflict alternative therapies on her, I had unintentionally taken over her own independence in my fight to keep her here.

No one in academia can train you to care for a loved one who is passing. I was booked in at Dorothy House for a carer's course, but never got to it as Mum made a turn for the worse, so I had to learn on the job. My mum was loved by people around her, so we often had people popping in.

One special person was Tony, my Cousin Susan's husband. My mother's name was Dorothy. She was known as Dot. Cousin

Susan called her Gert Aunt Dot; it is a West Country thing. So Tony always called her Gert. Every day he popped my mother the *Daily Mail* in, which was a bone of contention between us until I was in it one day. A very old friend of mine who was in PR called me one day and said, "I have put you forward for a *Daily Mail* feature, they are looking for cleaners who are now successful." So off I went to London for an interview and photo shoot. I was interviewed by an intern reporter. If you read the *Daily Mail* they often have features with three of four women in an article, who they have given a makeover with some story. Well this was one of those. The young intern asked me how my life was different now I had a business, after being a cleaner?

I said well one of the things that is nice is we have a party in the paddock and my bank manager is in a band, he usually plays. We get a barrel of beer and I love it.

She asked me about my life before. I told her we used to have egg and chip weeks to save up for Angelique's piano lessons. I told them Adrian was forty-four when she asked. Some of the bits were true but they had changed the whole concept of me. I never mentioned champagne or canapés or 300 people or landscaped gardens. It is journalistic licence. When my mum read it she went mad, I was really upset. She said, "Did you say that?"

"Of course I didn't," I protested. "I just told them about a barrel of beer and our party in the paddock." I was quite upset about it. Then I shouted at her, "Now believe all what you read in the bloody *Daily Mail*." That was it. From then on we used to say it has to be true if it was in the *Daily Mail*. She believed me in the end. I steered clear from national media coverage after a couple of other experiences.

The article read: *ANNETTE MARTIN, 45, lives in a three-bedroom cottage in Bath with her partner Adrian, 34, a sales director, and children Angelique, 26, a marketing manager, and Dominic, 18, a photography student. She is the owner and director of Bath Aqua Glass. Annette says:*

Each summer, standing in my garden, surrounded by 300 family and friends, drinking champagne and eating canapés, I can never resist a laugh.

Here I am, having splashed out thousands on my annual summer party, without giving the cost a second thought. Even more incredible is that I'm hosting the party in the landscaped gardens of my own beautiful country cottage.

But 20 years ago, I couldn't even afford to have a friend over for frozen pizza; and all my clothes came from jumble sales.

I was a single mother – my marriage broke down a few years after the children were born – and the only job that left me with enough free time to look after the children was cleaning.

For almost ten years, I scoured newsagents' windows looking for 'cleaning lady wanted' adverts. I found enough work to keep us going and enable me to pay for my daughter's piano lessons, but, all the same, we were constantly broke.

If the children wanted anything extra, we used to have 'egg-and-chip weeks'. By eating eggs and chips for a whole week, we were able to save enough to treat ourselves to a trip to the theatre or the zoo.

We lived in a rundown Victorian house with wallpaper peeling off the walls, and I drove a Reliant Robin which I'd bought for fifty pounds. Life was pretty tough.

I often used to look longingly at women in the supermarket filling their trolleys to the brim with delicious food – and wish I had the money to do the same...

I am actually crying with laughter as I have just googled it to put in the book. It is total bol ** ks. It is so funny. Adrian loves it because it made him look like my toy boy. I was actually glad I was not a journalist if it meant lying about people. My fantasy at fifteen was reporting on world affairs not rubbish like that.

So when Tony turned up we would joke he had bought us the 'scroll of truth'. Mum loved the crossword, the stars and the health sections ironically. Tony always greeted Mum with 'hello Gert' and she would always flirt like mad with him.

Adrian was a star. He loved my mum, he even cut her toenails. She was moaning she could no longer cut her toenails so I offered. She looked at me. "You are joking, you are so bloody clumsy you'd cut my toes off," so Adrian offered. I think in the last part of her life he gave her love equal to a real husband in the spiritual sense. When he was cutting them you could see she felt loved and cared for. We had many a special evening. She would always say there is nothing on telly, let's talk. So we would talk.

She told us stories of her past. Every year she had a reunion with her friends that she was with in the GNTC (Girls National Training Corps), that was from the age of fourteen, and they still all met up every year. There was Jym (that is her nickname, Sheila) Pip, Jean, Ogger (nick name) Jean, and Cynthia. They were all really good friend they had been through a lot together.

Jym who we knew as Auntie Jym had helped my mother when my father left. We had some amazing Christmases with her. She has a great larger than life personality, she always called my mother Potty Dotty. She looked after my mother over the years and took her and Jean to Australia to visit her family.

Pip, who lived very close to Mum now, had hitched to Scotland with her as a teenager, which is a wonderful story. She popped in three to four times a week in my mum's last days.

Jean who lived in London spent a lot of time with Mum. They used to go to Whitstable on Saturdays. Jean would drive and Mum would make supper.

She told us stories of her childhood, of when her father was the Home Guard; he had been in the 1st World War as a prisoner. So he felt slightly superior to the others in the Home Guard. He hid in the hedge outside their house and when Mr Parsons walked up on his guard night he shouted, 'ACHTUNG!' Mr Parsons nearly had a heart attack and shouted, 'WHO GOES THERE?' Mum said Granddad was wetting himself laughing in the bushes, and walked out with his hands up. Mr Parsons was really angry.

It was then I realised where the story had come from. It has been passed down generation after generation. In the past great storytellers did not need to read or write, just tell a story just how it happened. If it was good someone would repeat it.

Mum loved sharing her life, it meant her life becoming important and it was, and us listening reinforced that.

We knew these nights would not last forever. Mum went even more downhill and she could not get downstairs. We put a video player in her bedroom and Adrian and I used to sit on the bed either side of her. We were watching the sitcom *Gavin and Stacy* as it had the West–London–Essex connection she loved, but fell asleep on my shoulder. She was so frail then. I had bathed her the night before and her bones were showing. I felt the same love that I did towards my babies: totally unconditional. I looked at Ade and said, "We should go."

She stirred and said, "No, stay watch more." She wanted our love and our body presence. I had a thought, I would remember this moment it was so special. She was engulfed by our love and that is where she should have been and not in a lonely hospital bed with her head against bars.

The night nurses were lovely. They trained me on caring. They were perfect and they joked with my mum, affectionately calling her Dot and treated her like a person who was living not a person who was dying. My cousin Susan visited regularly, she loved Gert Aunt Dot.

The doctor who was looking after my mother was an obvious academic. He came one day as I had written him a letter. I sent it without asking anyone to check it which is what I did normally. I was angry after doing a lot of research and speaking to some doctors. They were in my extended family. I had asked if a twisted gut had been left for too long would it have caused the bio ducts to be blocked and could it turn cancerous. The answer which came back was 'yes'.

So I wrote an angry dyslexic letter to the GP who had diagnosed my mother with anorexia. I told him of my findings and that we would never sue the NHS but I wanted him to be aware that if an elderly women who has severe nausea it is almost definitely not anorexia and he should take them seriously in future incidents.

This was the same doctor who was in charge of my mother's end of life care; he visited on this particular day. He informed me my mother was a miracle, she should have died nine months ago. I explained about the alternative medicine. He 'pooh-pooed' it. I told him I felt it an honour to be looking after her. He asked why I hadn't got better things to do. I told him that this was the best thing I could be doing in my life at the moment. He didn't understand. When he left Mum said, "I hope you did not upset the doctor," as she had them on a pedestal. I told her 'no' as I stood next to her bed staring out of the window seeing him drive away in his Porsche.

Mum got worse; she needed a catheter because her organs were starting to fail. It gave her relief but she became obsessed with it. I did not realise this. One day I bought her up a cup of tea and she said could she have a look at the cafeteria. I was confused, and she was getting angry, because I did not understand what she was saying. So to calm her I went and got the cafeteria (coffee percolator). She screamed at me when I entered the room with it. "You bloody fool, not that cafeteria the one down there," pointing at her catheter bag. We again cried with laughter.

One of the gifts from my mother was to laugh in adversity.

Being dyslexic and having to write an important letter about a miscarriage of justice of any sort is difficult. Anyone who is in an academic position will look down on letters which are not composed in a certain way. It is like a secret code that I know I will never get, which in some ways I do not want to get.

We carried on caring for my mum. I know that it was a path to her passing which was covered in love by all of our family. We were in a position to be able to do this.

Mum was getting worried about me caring for her and took up the offer from Dorothy House for a week in their hospice in Winsley for 12 July. I told her I was OK but she insisted. Jim was coming up, we were in a routine.

She looked very upset one morning and I asked her what was wrong. She said, "I know I promised you a rest but I don't want to go into Dorothy House. I feel I am too close; I want to die in my own home.

I held her hand and said, "You don't want to die in Dorothy House."

She chuckled look at me and said, "Do you mind?"

"No, Mum, you know we all want you to be at peace with where you are."

She then said, "I know I have been hard on you at times, but you are a good girl and I love you." That meant so much to me as I had irritated her with my clumsy dyspraxic ways. I had frustrated her with my no fear attitude to doing things. She then said, "You are chaotic but an excellent businesswoman. I wish I could have been one."

"Mum, you taught me, you brought us up on fresh air, bought your house and then bought and sold until you got this one. Who is the best budgeter in the world," I told her.

She looked at me with pride in her eyes, "I am a businesswoman."

"Yes, Mum, the best."

I then made the excuse of making a cup of tea and broke my heart in the kitchen. My real dad had left her penniless and she had fought through. He had sold our house to use the money to start afresh with another woman. She had struggled through. I was so proud of her and so happy to be her daughter, now I knew she loved me. My mum had understood me finally. She always used to say I got you Annette when I saw the Bridget Jones films. I had got a bit upset but I can see it now.

Mum then started to hassle me, as she had met Eddie Burkes my ghost-busting boss. She said, "I know he taught you to take people over I need to go. Come on, Annette, take me over, I am ready." She was ready but I wasn't ready to let her go. But I knew that was selfish. So I phoned my cousin Jimmy who had been a chief druid. I had never discussed anything with him, in fact I had not seen him for years. He used to babysit Jimmy and I in the '60s and he taught us to do the twist. Him and Mum had great philosophical talks together. I explained my mother was very near to the end of her life and she needed someone to take her over. I explained I could not do it so I asked him if he could. "Yes," he said. "I will be up tomorrow."

Jimmy came the next day. We put a ring of stones in the garden with a gap and we walked around it and called in the family who had passed to take my mum over. That day my mum asked what Uncle John was doing here, and mentioned her mum and dad so I knew they had come. The next morning, very early, she called my name for the last time and I ran into her room. "Call Angelique and Jim and Dom," I said to Adrian which he did. Angelique came straight round and Mum died in our arms. We gave her permission to go as she was hanging on for us. My mum had gone. Jim arrived just after.

I had finally been able to talk to her about the funeral towards the end; she thought she had to be cremated. I told her she could be buried in Corsham. "Can I?" she said with the innocence of a little girl. So we arranged a plot. My mother had died like a queen with her family around so Jim and I wanted her to have a queen's funeral. We arranged a horse and carriage and for people to meet at her house, then to walk behind it to the church. The undertaker had asked Lord Metheun if he would open the gates at Corsham

Court so the horse and carriage could go up the avenue of trees to the church. He agreed.

Vicars are so good now, they do not mind if you are not religious, and let you have humanistic ceremonies. My mum loved the poem 'IF' by Rudyard Kipling so we all read a verse. Then the horse and carriage was to go across the meadows of Corsham Court and we walked behind again. It was like a scene from *Larkrise to Candleford*. We then went to the cricket pavilion which Tony ran and had the wake. It was fit for a queen. We visit her grave often and have the poem 'IF' engraved on a piece of Bath Aqua and Bristol Blue glass.

My mother, being obsessed with the other side all her life, said she would find a way to let me know if I am doing the right things in life. Well my brother hit a spot of bother and I was helping him out. It was quite heavy as he had contracted Lymes disease and he was too ill to run his business. I was cooking after a day at Bristol Blue and called to my mother, in desperation. "If you are there let me know I am doing the right thing. Send me that twenty-five pound premium bond win. Two days later I got a twenty-five pound win. Adrian was witness to this so I know she is there. She has actually sent me two to date.

I handled my grief by throwing myself into work with Bath Aqua and extreme bed and breakfasting. Adrian and I bought Jim's share of the house as he needed the money.

So I let my mum's house out as well to guests. I had my own overspill house now. Some days I made up to fourteen beds. I used to talk to my mother whilst doing changeover, it was a good grief process for me. It was almost like I was still visiting her.

Adrian was still entertaining the Hens as Mr Darcy. He would come home exhausted. I would flippantly say, "Ade gets so tired doing hen parties." Now the jungle gossip drums of our village can get quite rife. We found out at a party. It was a sit down dinner to start at Kingsdown Golf Club and all couples were separated. I was sat with the husband of the wife Adrian was sat with. Simultaneously we were having the same conversation. Firstly, the husband said to me in a broad west country accent, "I've 'erd all bout the husband entertaining them there Hens," then he winked.

I said, "What are you talking about?"

"Well I 'erd you 'aves them fer B&B and 'e entertains them."

I realised then that people thought Adrian was servicing the Hens. I explained the scenario quite bluntly that Adrian was giving them a glass blowing demonstration dressed as Mr Darcy in our studio in Walcot Street and we offered only bed and breakfast and no added exrtas. Adrian was having the exact same conversation with his wife. The husband said, "I faught it was a bit liberal of ye."

My grief got easier as time went on, Suzanne, Jim's wife, stepped in to sort Jim's business as he was ill. She is amazing and doing a fantastic job.

We had relocated to Orange Grove from Broad Street in 1999 with a seventeen-year lease. Orange Grove had been fine because there was a drop off point for the coaches which arrived in Bath. But suddenly with no consultation one of the taxi drivers told the lady in the Mad Hatters tea shop next door, tauntingly, "You are all going to go out of business as the coaches are going, it is just going to be a taxi rank." We were livid as local councils are obliged to consult all affected parties on decisions of change. So we eventually got retrospective consultation. It was a complete waste of our time, nobody listened. The liberal democrat Roger Symmonds told me it was a single member decision and there was nothing we could do about it. One of the people along Orange Grove got very ill through stress. The evening of the council meeting came where we could all have our three minutes to speak. It was farcical. We all spoke about the effect on our businesses this decision would have and then they passed the moving of the coaches. I forgot all protocol. I was so angry I got up walked towards the door and shouted, "You will bankrupt us all," and slammed the door.

What to do? We all got together and put marketing schemes. Then I was walking through Abbey churchyard and I saw the chocolate shop was up for lease so I phoned the number and asked the price. I nearly fell over and asked the man how independent shops could exist with rents like that. Then I thought about it a bit more, phoned him back and asked to have a look at it.

I then spoke to Gary, my accountant, who crunched some numbers and said we could do it. The footfall is ten times more than Orange Grove. The three of us sat down and deliberated it and finally we put in an offer. We got accepted over national chains with higher offers because we were an independent business with a good track record and a local product actually manufactured in central Bath. It was a big move and a massive rent and rates hike but I thought you only live once, if you don't try you don't ever know. We moved into this beautiful new shop and have not looked back. It is right next to the Abbey. it has two entrances it is more like a gallery than a shop. We make our stained glass in the shop. We have a wonderful cellar with a Victorian fire range. Its first shopkeeper was a lady milliners, in fact we exposed the sign on the door which says purveyor of hats – mourning hats a speciality.

What to do with Orange Grove? We still had four years on the lease, that is when I became a reluctant vintage and antique dealer.

In the next chapter I have put in some guides for business and being dyslexic. I hope they help.

Chapter Eleven

Dyslexic Guide: Running Your Own Business

1. FIND YOUR PASSION. Business is about passion. You might say business sometimes appears soulless and fickle, but I think this is because some people's passion is purely the art of making money. My life has to have creativity in it. I am passionate about glass and what it does. The truth of colour it reflects, all of its mediums. The fact it fascinates me and is so important in our lives: to give us light in our houses through windows, lenses in our glasses, the silicon chip which gave us computers. Of course the best thing for me is we can fuse it, blow it and we can make it into wonderful works of art. Your passion can be anything but if you are going to create a business it is like having a child. You need to love it as it will cause you sleepless nights and take your tolerance levels to heights you did not know you have. It also goes through different growing pains and stages. Before I had a business like anyone else I daydreamed that it would be easy and I could float around doing what I wanted. It is the polar opposite. So before you enter into your world of business be prepared to give your life and soul to it or forget it as it will fail.

2. ONCE YOU HAVE FOUND YOUR PASSION, RESEARCH IT. If it is simply making money then perhaps you can research how people make money, i.e. buying and selling. This is the first business ever to exist, it started with bartering, then we developed money. You have lots of ways to do it. But if you make money reinvest it into your business do not spend it on yourself that is

the secret. Do not get a bit of money, feel good, and go out and buy something you have wanted because that money has then gone. If you want to make your business work reinvest, reinvest. If you have made a bit of money, use your recently learnt expertise. Use your expertise to make more money, use what works. The best businesses are built on passion, love and recognising your experiences. If you fail, that is also a gift. Look at why you failed, learn from it, it almost has a greater value than success. Turn failure into success.

3. IF YOUR BUSINESS IS STARTING TO TAKE OFF YOU WILL NEED ORGANISATION. You need to keep all you receipts for purchases (things you buy for the business). Do not think that your time is free, log the time you are spending on the business (this is to measure the success you are achieving), put a wage figure against yourself from the beginning, you probably will not be receiving it. Also when it starts to take off make sure you have budgeted for staff which will give a true picture of your business profit and loss accounts. That is a record of what comes in and what goes out.

Most businesses take at least two years before going into profit, so find other means of funding your frugal lifestyle as unless you are wealthy in your own right it will be though. If you are new to business and are depending on your abilities, please set up an accounts package. There are lots on the internet. Find the one that suits your business, if you can enter and understand it yourself all well and good. But it you cannot, find a friend or family member who can. Use people, they are only to happy to help but find a way to reward them as nothing is free. Be at all times on top of you accounts and understand them. ALWAYS KNOW WHERE YOU ARE FINANCIALLY or get out of business, otherwise you will leave yourself open to theft or financial disaster. A dyslexic can always find a way to understand things and your accounts are the most important. They are the engine of your business, if the engine is not getting fuel (money in) it will cease to go forward and end up in the scrap yard. (In the hands of the bailiffs.)

3. TAKING ON STAFF. If your business starts to be unmanageable on your own and you have minimal wage from yourself coming from it, look at your forward prospects. Can you take a member of staff on? The question you need to ask is will that member of staff pay for their wage and make you a profit. If so recruit carefully. It is hard to find good staff because people always give you good impressions on an interview and often believe they can do anything even if they have had no experience. If you have read the beginning of this, my storybook, I was the perfect example of that. They are not your friend they are an employee. Employees who work with you for years and years become friends because your relationship has been tried and tested through trying times. But new staff are not your friends please remember this. It is business, you are asking them to perform duties for you, to go forward in your business in return for a wage. That is all. Your passion will be driving your business, whatever it is, and you would have put a lot of unpaid time and energy into it. So we always adopt a 'try before you buy' time. This is employing someone for a day or three day trial and assessing their abilities and finding out if they suit both parties. Your first employee on my advice should be a non-dyslexic. You must pay them on their trial days and give a letter stating this is the intention, making it legal. It is good for them and for you.

Unfortunately with us dyslexics it is all in our heads. So directing your employee can be difficult. I have had many a frustrating experience. I once had verbally given an employee a task. Then returning to ask whether it had been performed, they have on several occasions denied me ever saying it. So a suggestion to get round this, when you have recruited successfully, is to have a weekly meeting, where your employee takes minutes and lists your tasks you have visualised, then types this out and gives you a copy and also files a copy and keeps a copy themselves. Each week without fail you return to the task list and check it has been done, then create a new one. If things have not been done, find out why. Please add them to this week's task list to be ticked off next week.

I have learnt this through failures. In the past when I have told people verbally I would like tasks carried out and they denied me ever saying it. It has delayed the task being done and holds the business back. That also creates animosity. Also this can be used elsewhere, if you out source or subcontract using specialist or self-employed one-man bands. Always when you meet with them record your meeting, get them to take the minutes and email you a copy. People use your dyslexia as an excuse sometimes to cover their own mistakes.

In the past human resources were known as the personnel department. There is a code of conduct in employing staff and a lot of legal minefields. You can use the ACAS site on line if you have few employees, they are helpful. If you are growing successfully quite quickly you can outsource your HR to a company who will take a monthly fee and work closely on contracts for employees and your can also insure against legal situations with them. If you are still small the Federation of Small

Businesses offer a membership which gives you advice and a legal hot line.

4. IF YOUR BUSINESS IS GROWING A BIT MORE YOU WILL NEED AN ACCOUNTANT. This is an interesting one. I, being dyslexic, thought everyone knew better than me, one would have thought. Get rid of that thought, they are not. I will tell the story of my experience, please learn from this chapter. My business took off so I needed an accountant. I went through several. I was in awe of them as I thought they were so clever. Every time I interviewed a new one I would say 'I need to know what my accounts are saying. Will you teach me to read them?' Accounts become more and more complicated as your business grows. The reassuring 'yes' led me to take them on. I had also been honest and said that I needed it in layman's terms because I am dyslexic. After taking them on they always avoided telling me. So I got angry, sacked another one and then the penny dropped. I am paying for their service, so I decided to interview seven of them, perhaps I could find one I could work with. It was interesting. six of them were the same as the others and assured me in an aloof manner that they would show me; suffice to say I did not believe them. The third one was Gary, bingo he related to me. He told me he grew up with a small farm business and had taken himself off to train and through hard work and tenacity he qualified. He then and there asked me if I wanted to go through the set of accounts I had given him to show me the basics, which he did. We have worked closely together for five years now, not always perfect but it is a working relationship where we iron things out.

As your business grows you get new challenges. Choose your accountant carefully. Interview lots of them, business is about relationships. When you take on an accountant you will probably be a sole trader. Ask them what is best for your business – to be a limited company or if you are in partnership a partnership. They will explain the benefits of each one to your business. Also Google it. If your accountant is worth his weight he should not charge you to pick up the phone to ask questions. He will know your questions will be business growth information which will benefit him in the long run. Which means he has faith in you and your business. You need a good relationship with him and your bank manager.

5. CHOOSING A BANK. When you choose a bank choose carefully, ask people you know in business about their experience with their banks. Do your own surveys. Google the best banks for business. Insist on a relationship manager, do not enrol without one. You may not need one now but when the times get hard you will need a relationship to get through. Try to keep your credit rating good at all times. Remember be as independent as possible as banks give you umbrellas in sunshine and take them away when it is raining. They work very much on your credit scoring so keep a good credit score.

Riding bad times. Banks are a business like you, you are their customer they forget this sometimes. Remember they are not doing you a favour, you are a paying customer. You as a business customer pay more than ordinary customers.

I have been through several bad times as have many successful businesses. Things are always changing. Markets go up and down, economies change. So be prepared for a downturn in business.

Use credit cards always. Get a good credit rating with them and build up your lending power. Only use them cleverly, do not spend irrationally on them. They saved my business in hard times, when the banks were not lending. Yes I paid high rates but it gave me capital to steer my business through hard times. They were like the dinghies that saved us. Always work out payment plans so you pay back the quickest you can, therefore reducing the interest costs of them. Balance transfers are good, getting interest free periods. Please note there is always a fee but work out whether it is cheapest to transfer or stay.

Banks do not lend in a recession unless you have a business which is in lots of profit. Usually you are running with losses in a recession. Do not be afraid. What goes down must come up. The most guaranteed thing is change. If you believe your business will rise with the economy, fight for it. Beg steal and borrow. But always have a payment plan to pay back. Also read all of Richard Branson's and other business people's books, he too has been through interesting times. Audio books are available.

6. CHOOSE WHERE YOU ADVERTISE CAREFULLY. As a dyslexic we normally have a creative brain, you should be quite good at this. Do not do boring adverts: they do not work. Check which advertising is working. In today's market it is social media. Internet marketing is leading to results. If you are reading this in 2025 it will be totally different keep up with the changes. The basics do not change. Try to be different, you are unique. Look at what you notice when you are alerted to adverts. Most of all copy the big boys; they pay a lot of money to experts. If you can mimic something without plagiarising that's fine.

7. SIGNING DOCUMENTS. Please, please be careful, being dyslexic the last thing you can do is read a document, so get someone else to read it and highlight the areas that are questionable. Even get someone to record it so you can listen and make a judgement. I have been bitten too many times with this. It is a vulnerable area for dyslexics. Be strong, you do not have to sign anything without approving it in life.

8. ENJOYING YOUR BUSINESS. You will have ups and downs, but make sure you are enjoying your business. If it is getting you down, check if you can sell it. Sometimes people reach a point where they need a new passion. So ask your accountant if it has a value and look into it. If you are still in love with your business do get a work life balance. I needed to work on that as dyslexics can have tunnel vision.

9. HIPPY THOUGHTS IN BUSINESS. Always start your business with a new moon so it can grow with it.

Money is just energy passing through you, treat it with respect and wisdom and share it with charitable organisations you know are genuine, it will always come to you.

Love all, trust a few, always paddle your own canoe. Do not blame others for your mistakes. You are the leader of this business.

Do not obsess about your competitors, just travel your own line and keep it fresh.

Always be fair and kind to your staff, but strong if they are not performing. A member of staff must pay for themselves.

Most of all trust your gut. That is what it is there for.

Chapter Twelve

Summing up the 1970s and 2015.

I have spoken and interviewed several students who are dyslexic who have had similar experiences to myself and Tilly, my niece.

Interview with my niece.

Matilda, my niece, has very similar dyslexic traits to me. She is suffering almost identical experiences at school as I did.

Interview on 10-1-2015.

I asked how dyslexia had affected her.

Last year, 2014, when Matilda started her English class her teacher was not informed that she was dyslexic. She used to make Tilly read things in front of the class, and Tilly's stomach would drop and she wanted to cry. She used to beg the teacher not to make her read and it ended up with her running out of the class. She ended up after class taking responsibility on herself for letting the teacher know she was dyslexic. The teacher was surprised as it was not on any of her records, and Matilda appeared bright intelligent and self-confident. After she knew she would ridicule Tilly and other dyslexics about spelling mistakes. If she walked around the class when they were writing an essay Tilly would feel sick as the teacher would read the work and sneer if there were mistakes. Tilly said that she used to put examples on the board of a star of the class writings and belittle us if we did not come up to that standard. Sometimes Tilly could not understand the teaching language which frustrated her and would result in her getting angry and walking out of the class. She could not get the teachers to understand her inability to understand what they were saying. The reason she got angry is because she did not know what to do which made her feel stupid. Which like me she is far from.

Matilda in junior school was a great communicator but unable to write and spell, she was ridiculed by the other children and nicknamed 'special needs'.

Matilda's science teachers have always bothered, even helping with writing notes which reflected in her marks and she did better. She actually enjoyed science.

I asked Matilda how school has been for her. She said, "It's like walking barefoot through hot coals, hopefully in the future by the time I grow up and have kids the world will have a better understanding of dyslexia so my kids don't have to suffer what me and you did." That is exactly what I hoped for my children. In fact my son did really well and achieved good results because of a wonderful input from the teaching staff but not all schools operate like this.

In this day and age of technology and understanding, no matter how many times a dyslexic learns spellings they cannot put them into long-term memory. I learnt my spellings in junior school each week and got seven out of ten. At the end of the month when we had the test of all of them learnt that month I got naught out of ten. My teacher sent me outside the door. The headmaster came along and asked me why I was there. I told him. I was then sent to his office and caned on my hand. No wonder I had self-loathing when I write.

It would not be difficult to create alternative exams for dyslexics to show their skills. We are creative and the very fact that we could get good marks and not be put down would help us have confidence to go out into the outside world and succeed.

I learnt very quickly when I joined the recruitment agency that the students who are top of the class are not necessarily intelligent, they might just have photo recall. When I was in this position I interviewed people with top degrees. I found some of them had no common sense. I had to show them how to interview, I actually felt sorry for them.

Dyslexia in my family is prevalent, my brother, his daughter myself and my son have it so I googled 'is dyslexia passed down through the family?' It is thought if you have dyslexia there is a good chance your offspring will inherit the condition. If one identical twin is born with dyslexia, it is very likely the other twin will also have it.

I have written this in my own words.

Suggested Causes of dyslexia

The theories about the causes of dyslexia are genetic in many families. In some research it has been shown there are six genes that show up as a contribution to the dyslexic condition. In research it shows four genes affect neuronal migration. This is part of the process in the brain's development and specialised functions develop in a different way.

Research which has looked into brain scans show differences in the occipito-temporal cortex at the back of the brain. This is called 'phonological processing', which is thought to contribute to dyslexia

Phonological processing

The most widely supported theory of how dyslexia affects reading and writing is known as the 'phonological processing impairment theory'. To better understand this theory, it is useful to distinguish between how spoken and written language are understood.

The ability to understand spoken language seems to be a natural capacity of the human brain. This is why children as young as three years old can often speak and understand relatively complicated sentences.

As a result of this natural ability, when we listen to spoken language, we do not register that a word is made up of phonemes (the smallest units of sound that make up words). We only hear the word itself.

For example, when you hear the word 'crocodile', you hear it as one word. You do not have to break up the word into its phonemes and then reassemble them to make sense of it (which would be the sounds 'crok', 'o', 'dyle').

The same is not true of reading and writing. Both these skills require the ability to first recognise the letters in a word, then use these letters to identify the phonemes and assemble them to make sense of the word.

This ability is known as phonological processing. It is thought that people with dyslexia find phonological processing much more difficult than other people, because their brains function in a different way.

So with all this knowledge surely we can work out an exam system to measure our fantastic talents and direct us to the right careers? I am asking that question of the academics who try to fit square pegs in a round hole. We need a square hole: a set of exams which encourage our abilities.

The fact that a lot of people have been made to feel stupid because their brain works differently leads to unnecessary unemployment, lack of self-esteem and self-loathing. This affects every area of your life. Fortunately I was a confident soul in other parts of my life and a dreamer which is now recognised as positive affirmation, this was my saving grace. Not everyone has confidence and those people go into a shell and have a very disappointing life. So if you are a teacher and there is someone in your class who can't seem to get things right, irritates you, yes, irritates you (I irritated many teachers), have a heart to look at why that is. Do not ever make a dyslexic read out in class if they are not willing. Do not make an example of their work. Do look at the content of their work not the writing or the spelling. Most of all encourage them to do their work and mark them accordingly. Both Tilly and I became past masters of never giving work in as we did not want the negative response to our work. We both found detention easier.

I would welcome working with a government project to create a new system to teach and examine dyslexics. We have entrepreneurial qualities which creates business both SMEs and multi-national. Let's invest in the other side of the brain. It makes sense, it would create jobs and take people who falsely think they're dumb off the dole, a win win.

The end of my book... Hopefully a new beginning in education.